Contents

Cheese-stuffed garlic dough balls with a tomato sauce dip

Prep:40 mins **Cook:**35 mins plus at least 2 hrs-2 hrs 30 mins proving

Makes 20 - 25

Ingredients

- 50g butter , cubed
- 300g strong white bread flour
- 7g sachet fast-action dried yeast
- 1 tbsp caster sugar
- 200g block mozzarella , cut into 1.5cm cubes
- 65g gruyère , coarsely grated (optional)

For the garlic butter

- 100g butter
- 2 garlic cloves , crushed
- 1 rosemary sprig, leaves picked and finely chopped

For the tomato sauce dip

- 1 tbsp olive oil , plus extra for the bowl and baking sheet
- 1 garlic clove , sliced
- 250g passata
- 1 tsp red wine vinegar
- 1 tsp caster sugar
- pinch of chilli flakes
- ½ small bunch of basil , torn, plus extra to serve

Method

STEP 1

Heat 175ml water in a saucepan until steaming, then add the butter. Remove from the heat and leave to cool until the mixture is just warm (it should not be hot). Combine the flour, yeast, sugar and 1 tsp salt in a large bowl or stand mixer. Add the cooled butter mixture, and mix to a soft dough using a wooden spoon or the mixer. Knead for 10 mins by hand (or 5 mins using a mixer) until the dough feels bouncy and smooth. Transfer to an oiled bowl and cover with a clean tea towel. Leave somewhere warm to rise for 1½-2 hrs, or until doubled in size. Alternatively, leave to prove in the fridge overnight.

STEP 2

Oil and line a baking sheet with baking parchment. Knock the air out of the dough, then knead again for several minutes. Flatten a small piece of dough (about 20g) into a disc, and put a cube of the mozzarella and a pinch of the gruyère into the middle of the disc. Enclose the cheeses with the dough, then roll into a ball. Transfer to the prepared baking sheet. Repeat with the remaining cheese and dough, placing the dough balls ½cm apart on the baking sheet – they should be just touching after proving. Cover with a clean tea towel and leave somewhere warm to rise for 30 mins.

STEP 3

Meanwhile, make the garlic butter. Melt the butter in a small pan over a low heat, then stir in the garlic and rosemary. Remove from the heat and set aside until needed. Heat the oven to 180C/160C fan/gas 4. Brush the risen dough balls with the garlic butter, then bake for 25-30 mins until the dough balls are cooked through and the middles are oozing.

STEP 4

While the dough balls are baking, make the tomato sauce dip. Heat the oil in a saucepan and fry the garlic for 30 seconds. Tip in the passata, vinegar, sugar and chilli flakes, and simmer for 10 mins until thickened. Season to taste and stir in the basil. Brush the warm dough balls with any remaining garlic butter, then serve with the tomato sauce dip on the side for dunking.

Amatriciana chicken traybake

Prep:15 mins **Cook:**1 hr

Serves 4

Ingredients

- 1 long red chilli
- 3 tbsp tomato purée

- 3 tbsp olive oil
- 3 garlic cloves
- 8 skinless chicken thighs
- 500g new potato
- 4 thyme sprigs
- 140g cubetti di pancetta (or smoked bacon lardons)
- 400g tomato, half cherry or baby plum, the rest is up to you - any larger ones halved
- green salad and bread, to serve (optional)

Method

STEP 1

Heat oven to 200C/180C fan/gas 6. Find a large roasting tin that will hold the chicken thighs and potatoes in a single layer. Halve the chilli, scrape out and discard the seeds if you don't like it too hot, and remove the stalk. Put in a small food processor or mini chopper with the tomato purée, olive oil and garlic. Whizz to a paste, then spread over the chicken. Add the chicken and potatoes to the tin with a good grinding of black pepper and some salt, then mix everything together well with your hands. Add the thyme and roast for 30 mins.

STEP 2

Stir in the pancetta and roast for 15 mins more, then add the tomatoes and roast for another 15 mins until the tomatoes have softened and the chicken is cooked. Serve straight from the pan and eat with a green salad and some bread, if you like, for mopping up the juices.

Vanilla panna cotta

Prep: 10 mins **Cook:** 5 mins plus chilling

Serves 4

Ingredients

- 2 ½ sheets gelatine
- 150ml milk
- 400ml double cream
- 60g caster sugar
- 1 vanilla pod, split lengthways
- fresh strawberries, to serve

- strawberry compote, to serve

Method

STEP 1

Add the sheets of gelatine to a bowl of cold water and soak for 5 mins.

STEP 2

Pour the milk and cream into a saucepan with the sugar and vanilla seeds (to scrape the seeds out of the pod, use the back of a knife). Stir to combine and bring to a simmer, then remove from the heat. Take the gelatine out of the cold water and squeeze out the excess, then add to the milk mixture. Stir until completely dissolved. Tip into four ramekins and place in the fridge to set for at least a couple of hours.

STEP 3

To serve, turn each ramekin upside-down onto a serving plate. If the panna cotta won't drop out, carefully dip the ramekin in a bowl of warm water to loosen it. Serve with a drizzle of strawberry compote and sliced fresh strawberries.

Fresh pasta

Prep:30 mins **Cook:**2 mins - 3 mins plus resting

Serves 8

Ingredients

- 300g '00' pasta flour, plus extra for dusting
- 2 eggs and 4 yolks, lightly beaten
- semolina flour, for dusting

Method

STEP 1

Put the flour in a food processor with ¾ of your egg mixture and a pinch of salt. Blitz to large crumbs – they should come together to form a dough when squeezed (if it feels a little dry gradually add a bit more egg). Tip the dough onto a lightly floured surface, knead for 1 min or until nice and smooth – don't worry if it's quite firm as it will soften when it rests. Cover with cling film and leave to rest for 30 mins.

STEP 2

Cut away ¼ of the dough (keep the rest covered with cling film) and feed it through the widest setting on your pasta machine. (If you don't have a machine, use a heavy rolling pin to roll the dough as thinly as possible.) Then fold into three, give the dough a quarter turn and feed through the pasta machine again. Repeat this process once more then continue to pass the dough through the machine, progressively narrowing the rollers, one notch at a time, until you have a smooth sheet of pasta. On the narrowest setting, feed the sheet through twice.

STEP 3

Cut as required to use for filled pastas like tortellini, or cut into lengths to make spaghetti, linguine, tagliatelle, or pappardelle. Then, dust in semolina flour and set aside, or hang until dry (an hour will be enough time.) Store in a sealed container in the fridge and use within a couple of days, or freeze for 1 month.

Aperol spritz

Prep:5 mins No cook

Serves 2

Ingredients

- ice
- 100ml Aperol
- 150ml prosecco
- soda, to top up

Method

STEP 1

Put a couple of cubes of ice into 2 glasses and add a 50 ml measure of Aperol to each. Divide the prosecco between the glasses and then top up with soda, if you like.

Tomato & courgette risotto

Prep:10 mins **Cook:**25 mins

Serves 2

Ingredients

- 2 tbsp olive oil
- 1 small onion , diced
- 2 garlic cloves , crushed
- ½ tsp coriander seeds , crushed
- 200g risotto rice
- 500ml vegetable stock
- 200g carton passata
- 12 cherry tomatoes , halved
- 2 courgettes , halved and sliced
- 2 tbsp mascarpone
- parmesan (or vegetarian alternative), grated, to serve

Method

STEP 1

Put1 tbsp of oil in a large pan over a medium heat. Add the onion and cook for 5-7 mins until softened. Add the garlic and coriander seeds and cook, stirring, for another 1 min. Stir in the risotto rice, coating it in the onion mixture. Gradually add 300ml of the vegetable stock, stirring until fully absorbed by the rice between each addition. Pour the passata into the risotto, cover and simmer for 10-15 mins. Stir occasionally and add more stock as needed.

STEP 2

Meanwhile, heat oven to 200C/180C fan/gas 6. Put the cherry tomatoes and courgettes in a roasting tin, keeping them separate, drizzle with 1 tbsp olive oil, season and roast for 10-12 mins until just tender.

STEP 3

Add the mascarpone and plenty of seasoning to the risotto. Stir until the rice is completely cooked and the risotto is creamy, about 5 mins more. Add the courgettes and stir to combine. Serve the risotto in bowls topped with the roasted tomatoes and some grated Parmesan.

Fettuccine alfredo

Prep:15 mins **Cook:**10 mins

Serves 2 - 3

Ingredients

- 227g tub clotted cream
- 25g butter (about 2 tbsp)
- 1 tsp cornflour
- 100g parmesan, grated
- freshly grated nutmeg
- 250g fresh fettuccine or tagliatelle
- snipped chives or chopped parsley, to serve (optional)

Method

STEP 1

In a medium saucepan, stir the clotted cream, butter and cornflour over a low-ish heat and bring to a low simmer. Turn off the heat and keep warm.

STEP 2

Meanwhile, put the cheese and nutmeg in a small bowl and add a good grinding of black pepper, then stir everything together (don't add any salt at this stage).

STEP 3

Put the pasta in another pan with 2 tsp salt, pour over some boiling water and cook following pack instructions (usually 3-4 mins). When cooked, scoop some of the cooking water into a heatproof jug or mug and drain the pasta, but not too thoroughly.

STEP 4

Add the pasta to the pan with the clotted cream mixture, then sprinkle over the cheese and gently fold everything together over a low heat using a rubber spatula. When combined, splash in 3 tbsp of the cooking water. At first, the pasta will look wet and sloppy: keep stirring until the water is absorbed and the sauce is glossy. Check the seasoning before transferring to heated bowls. Sprinkle over some chives or parsley, then serve immediately.

Vegan pizza Margherita

Prep:15 mins **Cook:**15 mins plus rising and proving

Makes 2 large or 4 small pizzas (serves 4)

Ingredients

For the pizza dough

- 500g strong white bread flour, plus extra for dusting
- 1 tsp dried yeast
- 1 tsp caster sugar
- 1 ½ tbsp olive oil, plus extra

For the tomato sauce

- 100ml passata
- 1 tbsp fresh basil, chopped (or 1/2 tsp dried oregano)
- 1 garlic clove, crushed

For the topping

- 200g vegan mozzarella-style cheese, grated
- 2 tomatoes, thinly sliced
- Fresh basil or oregano leaves, chilli oil and vegan parmesan to serve (optional)

Method

STEP 1

Put the flour, yeast and sugar in a large bowl. Measure 150ml of cold water and 150ml boiling water into a jug and mix them together – this will mean your water is a good temperature for the yeast. Add the oil and 1 tsp salt to the warm water then pour it over the flour. Stir well with a spoon then start to knead the mixture together in the bowl until it forms a soft and slightly sticky dough. If it's too dry add a splash of cold water.

STEP 2

Dust a little flour on the work surface and knead the dough for 10 mins. Put it back in the mixing bowl and cover with cling film greased with a few drops of olive oil. Leave to rise in a warm place for 1 hr or until doubled in size.

STEP 3

Heat oven to 220C/200C/gas 9 and put a baking sheet or pizza stone on the top shelf to heat up. Once the dough has risen, knock it back by punching it a couple of times with your fist then kneading it again on a floured surface. It should be springy and a lot less sticky. Set aside while you prepare the sauce.

STEP 4

Put all the ingredients for the tomato sauce together in a bowl, season with salt, pepper and a pinch of sugar if you like and mix well. Set aside until needed.

STEP 5

Divide the dough into 2 or 4 pieces (depending on whether you want to make large or small pizzas), shape into balls and flatten each piece out as thin as you can get it with a rolling pin or using your hands. Make sure the dough is well dusted with flour to stop it sticking. Dust another baking sheet with flour then put a pizza base on top – spread 4-5 tbsp of the tomato sauce on top and add some sliced tomatoes and grated vegan cheese. Drizzle with a little olive oil and bake in the oven on top of your preheated baking tray for 10-12 mins or until the base is puffed up and the vegan cheese has melted and is bubbling and golden in patches.

STEP 6

Repeat with the rest of the dough and topping. Serve the pizzas with fresh basil leaves or chilli oil if you like and sprinkle over vegan parmesan just after baking.

Lighter chicken cacciatore

Prep:15 mins **Cook:**50 mins

Serves 4

Ingredients

- 1 tbsp olive oil
- 3 slices prosciutto, fat removed, chopped
- 1 medium onion, chopped

* 2 garlic cloves, finely chopped
* 2 sage sprigs
* 2 rosemary sprigs
* 4 skinless chicken breasts (550g total weight), preferably organic
* 150ml dry white wine
* 400g can plum tomatoes in natural juice
* 1 tbsp tomato purée
* 225g chestnut mushrooms, quartered or halved if large
* small handful chopped flat-leaf parsley, to serve

Method

STEP 1

Heat the oil in a large non-stick frying pan. Tip in the prosciutto and fry for about 2 mins until crisp. Remove with a slotted spoon, letting any fat drain back into the pan, and set aside. Put the onion, garlic and herbs in the pan and fry for 3-4 mins.

STEP 2

Spread the onion out in the pan, then lay the chicken breasts on top. Season with pepper and fry for 5 mins over a medium heat, turning the chicken once, until starting to brown on both sides and the onion is caramelising on the bottom of the pan. Remove the chicken and set aside on a plate. Raise the heat, give it a quick stir and, when sizzling, pour in the wine and let it bubble for 2 mins to reduce slightly.

STEP 3

Lower the heat to medium, return the prosciutto to the pan, then stir in the tomatoes (breaking them up with your spoon), tomato purée and mushrooms. Spoon 4 tbsp of water into the empty tomato can, swirl it around, then pour it into the pan. Cover and simmer for 15-20 mins or until the sauce has thickened and reduced slightly, then return the chicken to the pan and cook, uncovered, for about 15 mins or until the chicken is cooked through. Season and scatter over the parsley to serve.

Mozzarella peppers with chunky Italian dressing

Prep:5 mins **Cook:**20 mins

Serves 2

Ingredients

- 2 red peppers
- 5 sundried tomatoes , in olive oil
- handful good-quality olives
- 85g can anchovy , in oil
- small bunch basil , leaves torn
- 2 x 125g balls buffalo mozzarella , drained and halved
- balsamic vinegar
- selection of antipasti

Method

STEP 1

Heat oven to 220C/fan 200C/gas 7. Cut the peppers in half, scoop out the seeds and white membranes with a spoon and discard. Drizzle the peppers with a little olive oil from the tomato jar, rub all over and season generously. Roast for 20 mins until softened and starting to char.

STEP 2

Roughly chop the tomatoes and olives, then mix in a small bowl with 2 tbsp oil from the jar. Cut 4 anchovies lengthways, giving 8 thin strips, then add to the bowl along with the basil leaves. Season with black pepper. Keep the rest of the anchovies in an airtight container in the fridge for up to a week.

STEP 3

Take the peppers out of the oven and turn the grill to High. Pour any juice out of the peppers, then spoon in a little of the olive mix. Snuggle a mozzarella half into each pepper and return to the roasting tin. Grill for about 3 mins until the top of the cheese has just softened, but not melted. Put the antipasti on a serving platter and add the peppers. Spoon over the rest of the olive mix and splash with a little balsamic vinegar. Enjoy with bread and a glass of wine.

Roast red wine lamb with Italian beans

Prep: 15 mins **Cook:** 1 hr and 30 mins Plus reducing time for the gravy

Serves 8

Ingredients

- 2kg leg of lamb
- 4 garlic cloves , sliced
- 8 good sprigs thyme
- 5 tbsp olive oil
- half a bottle red wine
- zest 1 lemon
- 1l hot lamb stock
- 3 red onions , each cut into 6 wedges
- 2 tbsp balsamic vinegar

For the beans

- 2 rosemary , needless roughly chopped
- 100g SunBlush tomato , drained and roughly chopped
- 3 x 400g cannellini beans
- handful flatleaf parsley , roughly chopped

Method

STEP 1

Using a sharp knife, cut small slashes all over the lamb, then push a slice of garlic into each. Put half the thyme, 3 tbsp olive oil, wine, lemon zest and a good grinding of black pepper into a large freezer bag. Addthe lamb, tie the bag tightly and refrigerate for at least 4 hrs, preferably overnight.

STEP 2

Heat oven to 220C/fan 200C/gas 7. Put the rest of the thyme into the bottom of a roasting tin then lift the lamb out of the marinade and sit on top of the thyme. Roast for 20 mins, then toss onions into the pan, drizzle with a little oil, then turn the oven down to 190C/fan 170C/gas 5. Roast for 15 mins/450g for medium. Meanwhile, strain the marinade into a pan, add most of the stock and boil until reduced by two thirds (this will take about 20 mins). Set aside. Gravy can be made ahead or the day before if necessary, as long as the meat has marinated for 4 hrs.

STEP 3

Once the lamb is ready, take out and rest on a board, wrapped in a tent of foil to keep warm. Set the onions aside in a bowl. Put the roasting tin onto a low heat and add the balsamic vinegar to the tin with a splash more stock and scrape all the meaty bits from the bottom. Tip into the jug with the gravy.

STEP 4

For the beans, add 2 tbsp oil to the roasting tin. Add the rosemary and tomatoes, and fry for 1 min until the rosemary smells aromatic. Tip in the beans, the red onions and the final splash of stock, then warm through. Season, then stir in the parsley just before serving. Serve on a platter, topped with the lamb.

Ultimate spaghetti carbonara recipe

Prep:15 mins - 20 mins **Cook:**15 mins

Serves 4

Ingredients

- 100g pancetta
- 50g pecorino cheese
- 50g parmesan
- 3 large eggs
- 350g spaghetti
- 2 plump garlic cloves, peeled and left whole
- 50g unsalted butter
- sea salt and freshly ground black pepper

Method

STEP 1

Put a large saucepan of water on to boil.

STEP 2

Finely chop the 100g pancetta, having first removed any rind. Finely grate 50g pecorino cheese and 50g parmesan and mix them together.

STEP 3

Beat the 3 large eggs in a medium bowl and season with a little freshly grated black pepper. Set everything aside.

STEP 4

Add 1 tsp salt to the boiling water, add 350g spaghetti and when the water comes back to the boil, cook at a constant simmer, covered, for 10 minutes or until al dente (just cooked).

STEP 5

Squash 2 peeled plump garlic cloves with the blade of a knife, just to bruise it.

STEP 6

While the spaghetti is cooking, fry the pancetta with the garlic. Drop 50g unsalted butter into a large frying pan or wok and, as soon as the butter has melted, tip in the pancetta and garlic.

STEP 7

Leave to cook on a medium heat for about 5 minutes, stirring often, until the pancetta is golden and crisp. The garlic has now imparted its flavour, so take it out with a slotted spoon and discard.

STEP 8

Keep the heat under the pancetta on low. When the pasta is ready, lift it from the water with a pasta fork or tongs and put it in the frying pan with the pancetta. Don't worry if a little water drops in the pan as well (you want this to happen) and don't throw the pasta water away yet.

STEP 9

Mix most of the cheese in with the eggs, keeping a small handful back for sprinkling over later.

STEP 10

Take the pan of spaghetti and pancetta off the heat. Now quickly pour in the eggs and cheese. Using the tongs or a long fork, lift up the spaghetti so it mixes easily with the egg mixture, which thickens but doesn't scramble, and everything is coated.

STEP 11

Add extra pasta cooking water to keep it saucy (several tablespoons should do it). You don't want it wet, just moist. Season with a little salt, if needed.

STEP 12

Use a long-pronged fork to twist the pasta on to the serving plate or bowl. Serve immediately with a little sprinkling of the remaining cheese and a grating of black pepper. If the dish does get a little dry before serving, splash in some more hot pasta water and the glossy sauciness will be revived.

Marmite & pancetta spaghetti

Prep:5 mins **Cook:**10 mins - 12 mins

Serves 4

Ingredients

- 500g pack of spaghetti
- 1 tbsp olive oil
- 200g pancetta , diced
- 80g butter , softened
- 2 tsp Marmite
- 50g cheddar , grated
- grated parmesan , to serve

Method

STEP 1

Bring a large pan of water to the boil and add the spaghetti. Meanwhile, heat the oil in a frying pan and cook the pancetta for 8-10 mins until crispy.

STEP 2

Once the pasta is cooked, drain, reserving a little pasta water. Tip the spaghetti back into the pan with the pasta water and add the pancetta with the fat from the pan, the butter, Marmite and cheeses. Use tongs to coat the spaghetti in the sauce and season with a little pepper. Taste and add a little more Marmite , if you like. Serve in bowls with extra Parmesan sprinkled over.

Next level tiramisu

Prep:35 mins **Cook:**5 mins plus 3 hrs chilling

Serves 6

Ingredients

- 3 egg yolks
- 100g golden caster sugar , plus extra for the dish
- 1 tsp vanilla extract
- whole nutmeg , for grating
- 150ml marsala
- 250g tub mascarpone
- 300ml double cream
- 200ml strong black coffee , cooled
- 24 sponge fingers or savoiardi biscuits

For the topping

- 100g golden caster sugar
- 1 tsp fine espresso powder
- 1 tsp cocoa powder , plus extra for serving

Method

STEP 1

Beat the egg yolks, sugar, the vanilla, a grating of nutmeg and 50ml of the marsala using an electric whisk in a heatproof bowl over a pan of barely simmering water for 10 mins, until pale and light. Put in the fridge to cool.

STEP 2

In a separate bowl, beat the mascarpone and cream together with an electric whisk until the mixture holds soft peaks. Gently fold the egg yolk and cream mixtures together with a spatula, being careful not to over-stir. Put the bowl back in the fridge to chill.

STEP 3

Scatter a little sugar over the base of a deep 20 x 20cm serving dish. Pour the coffee and the remaining 100ml marsala into a bowl. One by one, dip 12 biscuits in the coffee mixture on each side for a couple of seconds (don't leave them too long or they'll go soggy), then lay flat in the dish to cover the base. Spread over half the cream mixture. Dip the remaining biscuits in the coffee and arrange on top of the cream, then finish with a final layer of the cream. Cover the dish and chill for at least 3 hrs. Can be made up to two days in advance.

STEP 4

To make the crunchy topping, put the sugar and a splash of water in a saucepan, and stir to combine. Simmer over a medium heat until you have an amber-coloured caramel. Pour the caramel onto a parchment-lined baking tray and tilt to spread. While it's still hot, dust with the coffee and cocoa powder, then leave to set until hard. Break into small pieces, then blitz in a processor to a rough crumb. Sprinkle over the tiramisu and dust with a little cocoa powder to serve.

Sausage, sweet potato & sweetcorn bake

Prep:5 mins **Cook:**50 mins

Serves 4

Ingredients

- 2 tbsp rapeseed oil
- 300g sweet potatoes , peeled and cut into wedges
- 2 corn on the cob , each cut into 3
- pinch chilli or barbecue spices (use more if you all like spice)
- 12 chipolata sausages
- 1 tbsp grated parmesan
- barbecue sauce , to serve

Method

STEP 1

Heat oven to 200C/180C fan/gas 6. Put 1 tbsp oil in a bowl, tip in the wedges and toss them in the oil along with some seasoning. Arrange them in the centre of a large baking tray. Tip the corn into the bowl with the remaining oil and some seasoning, and arrange them on one side of the wedges. Sprinkle some chilli or spices on one half of the wedges (do the whole lot if everyone likes spices). Arrange the sausages on the empty third of the tray.

STEP 2

Put the tray in the oven and cook for 40 mins, turning the sausages and corn over halfway through. Take the tray out of the oven and sprinkle the parmesan over the corn, put it back in the oven and cook for 10 mins. Serve with the barbecue sauce.

Amarena cherry & almond tart

Prep:30 mins **Cook:**50 mins plus resting

Makes 12 slices

Ingredients

- 125g butter
- 125g golden caster sugar
- 225g plain flour
- ½ egg or 1 egg yolk

For the frangipane filling

- 125g butter , at room temperature
- 125g golden caster sugar
- 3 medium eggs
- 1 lemon , zested
- 125g finely ground almonds or almond flour
- 120g Fabbri amarena cherries (see tip)
- icing sugar , for dusting (optional)

Method

STEP 1

Mix together the butter, sugar, flour, a pinch of salt and the egg in a food processor to make a dough, then wrap and leave to rest in the fridge for 30 mins. The dough should be cold but still easy to work with by the time you roll it out.

STEP 2

Meanwhile, make the frangipane filling. Melt the butter in a pan over a low heat, then set aside to cool slightly. Beat the sugar with the eggs and lemon zest in a bowl until creamy. Pour in the melted butter while continuing to beat, then add the ground almonds (or almond flour) and fold into the mixture. Heat oven to 175C/155C fan/gas 3½.

STEP 3

Line a buttered tart tin or ring mould (approximately 23cm) with the rolled-out pastry dough, then trim any overhanging edges. Spread the frangipane evenly into the tin and arrange the cherries on top with some of their syrup, so the top of the tart is covered in a thin layer.

STEP 4

Put the tart in the oven and bake for about 40-45 mins until golden brown, puffed and firm to the touch. Leave to cool on a rack. Dust with some icing sugar, if you like, before serving in slices.

Italian chickpea stew

Prep:40 mins - 50 mins **Serves 8**

Ingredients

- 550g salad potato (such as Charlotte)
- 250g bag trimmed, washed spinach leaves
- 4 tbsp light olive oil
- 1 red onion , finely chopped
- 2 garlic cloves , finely chopped
- ½ tsp dried crushed chilli
- 200ml dry white wine (2 small glasses)
- 6 plum tomatoes , peeled, seeded and diced
- 2x cans chickpea (preferably organic), drained and rinsed
- 2 tbsp lemon juice
- 6 tbsp chopped fresh parsley
- 2 tbsp chopped fresh mint
- 4 tbsp extra-virgin olive oil

Method

STEP 1

Cook the potatoes in salted boiling water for 15-20 minutes until tender. Meanwhile, tip the spinach into a colander or sieve, pour boiling water over it from the kettle so the spinach wilts, then hold it under the cold tap until it's cooled down. Shake it well and leave to drain. Drain the potatoes and cut into 1cm dice.

STEP 2

Heat the light olive oil in a large pan and cook the onion and garlic over a low heat for 3-4 minutes until soft and translucent. Add the chillies and wine, tip in half the tomatoes and cook over a moderate heat until nearly all the wine has evaporated. Stir in the chickpeas, diced potatoes and spinach and cook for 5 minutes.

STEP 3

Add the lemon juice, parsley, mint, extra virgin olive oil and remaining tomatoes. Season with salt and pepper to taste. If the stew seems a little dry, add a splash of water or vegetable stock.

Italian apricot fool

Total time40 mins Takes 30-40 minutes, plus cooling

Serves 6

Ingredients

- 500g ripe fresh apricots , halved and stoned
- finely grated zest and juice of 1 lemon
- 140g golden caster sugar
- 3 tbsp Cointreau or other orange flavoured liqueur
- 500g carton mascarpone
- 142ml carton double cream
- 18 amaretti biscuits , plus extra to serve

Method

STEP 1

Put the apricot halves in a saucepan with the lemon zest and juice and the sugar. Shake the pan to combine, then simmer, uncovered, over a medium heat until the apricots are soft. This should take about 10-15 minutes.

STEP 2

Tip the contents of the pan into a blender or food processor and whizz to a purée. Decant into a bowl, stir in the liqueur and leave to cool – about 20-30 minutes.

STEP 3

Soften the mascarpone in its tub by whisking it vigorously with a fork. Whip the cream in a bowl – you want it softly whipped not stiff. Fold in the mascarpone with a large metal spoon, then lightly swirl in the apricot purée to make a pattern.

STEP 4

Spoon the mixture into six wine glasses. (At this point, they'll keep in the fridge for up to a day.) To serve, crumble over the amaretti, with a few on the side for dunking.

Mushroom & spinach risotto

Prep:50 mins - 55 mins **Serves 2**

Ingredients

- 1 tbsp olive oil
- 25g butter
- 1 onion, chopped
- 140g chestnut mushrooms, sliced
- 1 fat garlic clove, crushed
- 140g arborio rice
- 150ml dry white wine
- 4 sundried tomatoes, chopped
- 500ml hot vegetable stock
- 2 tbsp chopped fresh parsley
- 25g parmesan or vegetarian alternative, freshly grated
- 100g fresh young leaf spinach, washed if necessary
- warm ciabatta and green salad, to serve

Method

STEP 1

Heat the oil and butter in a large deep frying pan. Add the onion and cook gently for 5 minutes until softened. Stir in the mushrooms and garlic and cook gently for 2-3 minutes.

STEP 2

Stir in the rice to coat with the onion and mushroom mixture. Pour in the wine and cook over a moderate heat for about 3 minutes, stirring from time to time, until the wine is absorbed.

STEP 3

Reduce to a gentle heat. Add the tomatoes and 125ml/ 4fl oz of the stock and cook for about 5 minutes until the liquid is absorbed. Pour in a further 125ml/4fl oz stock and continue cooking until absorbed. Repeat with the remaining stock, until it is all absorbed and the rice is creamy and tender.

STEP 4

Stir in the parsley and half the parmesan. Season to taste. Scatter the spinach over the risotto. Cover and cook gently for 4-5 minutes until the spinach has just wilted. Serve immediately sprinkled with the remaining parmesan.

Gluten-free pizza dough

Prep:20 mins **Serves 4**

Ingredients

- 400g gluten-free bread flour
- 2 heaped tsp golden caster sugar
- 2 tsp gluten-free baking powder
- 1 tsp fine salt
- 1 heaped tsp xanthan gum
- 5 tbsp olive oil

Method

STEP 1

Mix the flour, sugar, baking powder, salt and xanthan gum in a large mixing bowl. Make a well in the centre and pour in 250ml warm water and the olive oil. Combine quickly with your hands, to create a thick, wet, paste-like texture, adding an extra 20ml warm water if the dough feels a little dry. Store in an airtight container or covered bowl in the fridge for up to 24 hours before using.

Salted caramel pear cake

Prep:1 hr **Cook:**50 mins

Serves 12

Ingredients

- 2cm piece ginger , grated
- 4 Williams pears , 3 grated over a sieve, reserving the pear juice for the caramel, 1 peeled, cored and chopped (do this when about to decorate)
- 360g self-raising flour
- 15g rye flour
- 1 tsp ground ginger
- ½ tsp turmeric
- ½ tsp nutmeg
- ½ tsp ground cardamom
- ½ tsp cinnamon
- 1 tsp baking powder
- 4 eggs
- 200g golden caster sugar
- 150g light brown muscovado sugar , sieved
- 150ml rapeseed or vegetable oil
- 120g natural yogurt
- toasted buckwheat , dehydrated pear and rosemary, to serve (optional)

For the pear-salted caramel

- 50g unsalted butter , plus extra for the tins
- 50ml reserved pear juice
- 150ml perry
- 100g light brown muscovado sugar
- 1 tbsp double cream
- generous pinch sea salt

For the icing

- 4 egg whites
- 250g golden caster sugar
- 250g butter , at room temperature
- 2 tbsp tahini
- 1 tbsp vanilla bean paste

Method

STEP 1

Heat oven to 195C/175C fan/gas 5 ½. Butter and line the base of three 20cm round cake tins. Add the grated ginger to the grated pear and push down with a wooden spoon to squeeze out as much juice as possible.

STEP 2

Mix the flours, spices, baking powder and 1 tsp salt in a bowl. In a stand mixer, vigorously whisk the eggs and sugars for 3 mins until thick and frothy. Slowly pour in the oil in a steady stream. Turn the speed down, then add the flour mixture, 2 tbsp at a time, alternating with the yogurt, until incorporated. Mix in the grated pear (for no longer than 20 secs). Divide the mixture between the tins and bake for 25-30 mins or until a skewer inserted comes out dry.

STEP 3

For the caramel, heat the pear juice and perry in a pan until reduced to about 50ml. Add the sugar and butter and whisk to a smooth caramel, then add the cream and whisk again until smooth. Add sea salt to your taste – I'd go for a generous pinch, so that the caramel is still fruity and sharp but has a little saltiness to it – then allow to cool slightly to just warmer than room temperature.

STEP 4

To make the buttercream, put the egg whites and sugar in the bowl of a stand mixer. Place the bowl over a pan of boiling water, then whisk until the sugar dissolves and the mixture is no longer gritty. Put the bowl in the mixer, then whisk until soft peaks form and the bowl returns to room temperature. Switch to the paddle attachment, then add the butter, one spoonful at a time. Add the tahini, vanilla and a pinch of salt, and beat to a light, fluffy icing.

STEP 5

Place the bottom layer of sponge on a platter or cake stand, then top with a layer of the buttercream and scatter over a third of the chopped pear. Repeat with the next two layers. To ice the cake, do an intial layer all over, chill in the fridge for 20 mins, then use the remaining icing to cover everything. Use a stepped spatula to spread it out evenly. Pour the caramel over the top of the cake, and allow it to drip down the sides. Scatter with toasted buckwheat, dehydrated pear and rosemary, if you like.

Pesto & goat's cheese risotto

Prep:2 mins **Cook:**30 mins

Serves 2

Ingredients

- olive oil , for frying
- 200g risotto rice
- 700ml chicken stock or vegetable stock
- 1 tub fresh pesto
- 100g soft goat's cheese

Method

STEP 1

Pour a glug of olive oil into a large saucepan. Tip in the rice and fry for 1 min. Add half the stock and cook until absorbed. Add the remaining stock, a ladle at a time, and cook until the rice is al dente, stirring continually, for 20-25 mins.

STEP 2

Stir through the pesto and half the goat's cheese. Serve topped with the remaining cheese.

Tagliata & borlotti beans

Prep:15 mins **Cook:**5 mins

Serves 2

Ingredients

- small bunch parsley
- ½ small bunch basil
- 1 small garlic clove
- 3 tbsp olive oil , plus a drizzle
- 1 tbsp red wine vinegar
- 250g rump steak , about 2cm thick
- 400g can borlotti beans , drained and rinsed
- 50g rocket
- 80g cherry tomatoes , halved
- 25g parmesan , shaved (optional)

Method

STEP 1

Put the parsley, basil, garlic, olive oil and 1 tbsp water in the small bowl of a food processor and whizz until the herbs are finely chopped. Transfer to a bowl, stir through the vinegar and season to taste.

STEP 2

Season the steak generously. Heat a griddle pan or non-stick frying pan over a high heat. Drizzle a little extra oil over the steak and fry for 5 mins, turning every minute. Put on a plate, cover and leave for about 5 mins to rest.

STEP 3

Toss the beans, rocket and cherry tomatoes in the herb mixture. Slice the steak into strips. Divide the salad between two plates, top with the steak and scatter over the shaved parmesan, if you like.

Baci di dama

Prep:15 mins **Cook:**20 mins Plus chilling and setting

Makes 16 biscuits

Ingredients

- 100g blanched hazelnuts , toasted
- 100g butter

- 100g caster sugar
- 100g flour (preferably '00' flour)

For the filling

- 100g dark chocolate , broken into small pieces

Method

STEP 1

Blitz the hazelnuts to fine crumbs, but be careful not to over-blitz – you don't want them to become oily. Add the butter and sugar, and blitz again until really creamy, then tip the mixture into a bowl and sift in the flour. Mix with your hands, then chill in the fridge for an hour or until firm enough to roll.

STEP 2

Heat oven to 180C/160C fan/gas 4 and line a large baking sheet with baking parchment. Tear off teaspoon-sized chunks of mixture and roll into balls, then place on the lined sheet around 2 cm apart. Bake for 15 mins until golden brown, then transfer to a wire rack to cool.

STEP 3

To make the filling, heat the chocolate in a bowl in the microwave, stirring every 10 secs until fully melted. Spread a small spoonful of chocolate on half the cooled biscuits. Leave to set for 15 mins then sandwich the remaining biscuits on top. Leave the baci di dama to set completely (put them in the fridge if the kitchen is warm). Serve with coffee.

Mozzarella, pepper & aubergine calzone

Prep:15 mins **Cook:**35 mins

Serves 4

Ingredients

- 400g strong wholewheat bread flour , plus extra for dusting
- ⅛ tsp salt (optional)
- 7g sachet fast-action dried yeast

- 2 tsp rapeseed oil , plus extra for the baking sheet

For the filling

- 2 tsp rapeseed oil
- 1 red and 1 yellow pepper , deseeded and cut into small chunks
- 1 large aubergine , halved lengthways and thinly sliced
- 2 large garlic cloves , finely chopped
- 1 tbsp tomato purée
- 1 tbsp balsamic vinegar
- small bunch basil , roughly torn
- 8 pitted Kalamata olives , halved
- 125g ball mozzarella (drained weight), quartered
- milk or beaten egg, for brushing

Method

STEP 1

Put the flour, salt (if using), yeast, oil and 300ml lukewarm water in a bowl and mix until soft. Knead into a ball (try not to add any extra flour) – it will be sticky but the flour will absorb some moisture. Return to the bowl, cover and leave somewhere warm.

STEP 2

Meanwhile, make the filling. Heat the oil in a large non-stick pan, then stir-fry the peppers for about 1 min until they start to soften. Add the aubergine and garlic and continue to cook over a medium heat for 8-10 mins, gently pressing the veg with a wooden spoon until it breaks down a little. If it doesn't, fry, covered, for a few extra mins.

STEP 3

Stir in the tomato purée, vinegar and 2 tbsp water. When the veg is soft, remove the pan from the heat and stir through the basil.

STEP 4

Heat the oven to 220C/200C fan/gas 7. Quarter the risen dough and roll each piece out to a 20cm circle on a lightly floured surface. Spoon a quarter of the filling over one side, scatter over a quarter of the olives, top with a quarter of the cheese, and brush the edges with the milk or beaten egg. Fold the dough over the filling and pinch the edges together at the side, a bit like making a Cornish pasty. Lift onto a lightly oiled baking sheet and brush with more milk or beaten egg. Repeat with the remaining dough and filling to make four calzones, then bake for 15-20 mins until golden. Leave to cool slightly and serve at room temperature.

Creamy courgette risotto

Prep:20 mins **Cook:**35 mins

Serves 3 - 4

Ingredients

- 50g butter, plus 2 knobs more
- 1 small onion, finely chopped
- 250g courgette, 140g coarsely grated, the rest diced
- 175g risotto rice
- zest and juice 1 lemon
- 1.2l vegetable (or chicken) stock, kept hot on a low heat
- 25g parmesan (or vegetarian alternative), grated
- 2 heaped tbsp mascarpone
- splash of olive oil
- 1 heaped tbsp toasted pine nuts

Method

STEP 1

Melt the butter in a sturdy frying pan, add the onion and gently fry until softened. Stir in the grated courgettes and rice, increase the heat and sizzle while stirring for 1-2 mins.

STEP 2

Add the lemon juice and a ladle of hot stock, and bubble over a medium-high heat while stirring constantly. When the liquid has just about been absorbed, add another ladleful of stock. Keep cooking like this for 20-25 mins until the rice is just tender and is creamy. Stir in the Parmesan, mascarpone and some seasoning, cover with a lid or baking sheet, and set aside for 5 mins while you cook the remaining courgettes.

STEP 3

Heat the remaining butter and a splash of oil in a small frying pan. Add the diced courgettes, and fry over a high heat for 2-3 mins until golden and just softened. Divide the risotto between shallow bowls or plates, then scatter with the diced courgettes and any buttery juices, the pine nuts and a few pinches of lemon zest.

Italian-style bass

Prep:6 mins - 10 mins **Cook:**15 mins

Serves 6

Ingredients

- 750g waxy potato , such as Charlotte
- 6 sea bass fillets, skin on, 175-200g each
- 250g pack cherry tomato
- handful black Italian olives
- 4-5 tbsp fish stock (preferably from the chiller cabinet)
- 4-5 tbsp dry white wine
- basil , to serve

Method

STEP 1

Heat oven to 190C/fan 170/gas 5. Slice the potatoes and boil for 6-8 mins until just tender, then drain.

STEP 2

Butter or oil one large or two smaller shallow ovenproof dishes that will fit the fish fillets in one layer (a couple of roasting tins would work well). Scatter the potatoes over the base of the dishes, then halve the tomatoes and scatter on top, along with the olives. Set the fish fillets among the other ingredients then pour over the stock and wine, then season to taste.

STEP 3

Cover the dishes with foil and seal the edges. Bake for 15 mins until the fish is tender. Serve each portion on warm plates and scatter with basil.

Winter panzanella

Prep:15 mins **Cook:**45 mins

Serves 4

Ingredients

- 1 cauliflower , broken into florets
- 100ml extra virgin olive oil
- 250g good bread, such as sourdough or ciabatta
- 2 red chillies , halved, deseeded and finely chopped
- 4 garlic cloves , finely sliced
- 8 anchovies , finely chopped
- 35g raisins , soaked in just-boiled water and drained
- 1 tbsp capers , rinsed of salt or brine
- 4 tbsp roughly chopped flat leaf parsley
- 5 radishes (preferably French breakfast radishes), finely sliced
- 1 tsp white balsamic vinegar or white wine vinegar
- juice of ½-1 lemon

Method

STEP 1

Steam the cauliflower until it's just tender (be careful not to overcook it), then set aside.

STEP 2

Tear the bread into small chunks and heat 3 tbsp of the olive oil in a large frying pan. Fry the bread over a medium heat (in batches if it's easier) until it's golden all over – each batch will take about 4-5 mins to get a good colour. Put all the bread back into the pan and add the chilli, garlic and anchovies to the pan (with another tablespoon of oil if necessary) and sauté for a further 2 mins, making sure the garlic doesn't get too dark. It should be golden, not brown. Tip the bread mixture into a broad shallow serving bowl and add the raisins, capers and parsley.

STEP 3

Add the rest of the olive oil to the frying pan and, over a high heat, fry the cauliflower until tinged with gold. You want a really good colour. Put the cauliflower in the bowl with the bread mixture, add the radishes, balsamic vinegar and the juice of ½ lemon and toss everything together. Season, but be careful about how much salt you use because of the anchovies. Taste to see if you need more lemon juice, or even more olive oil, and serve warm.

Roasted vegetable lasagne

Prep:25 mins **Cook:**1 hr and 10 mins

Serves 6

Ingredients

- 3 red peppers, cut into large chunks
- 2 aubergines, cut into ½ cm thick slices
- 8 tbsp olive oil, plus extra for the dish
- ½ quantity tomato sauce (see below)
- 300g fresh lasagne sheets
- ½ quantity white sauce (see below)
- 125g ball mozzarella (or vegetarian alternative)
- handful of cherry tomatoes, halved

Method

STEP 1

Heat the oven to 200C/180C fan/gas 6. Lightly oil two large baking trays and add the peppers and aubergines. Toss with the olive oil, season well, then roast for 25 mins until lightly browned.

STEP 2

Reduce the oven to 180C/160C fan/gas 4. Lightly oil a 30 x 20cm ovenproof dish. Arrange a layer of the vegetables on the bottom, then pour over a third of the tomato sauce. Top with a layer of lasagne sheets, then drizzle over a quarter of the white sauce. Repeat until you have three layers of pasta.

STEP 3

Spoon the remaining white sauce over the pasta, making sure the whole surface is covered. Scatter over the mozzarella and cherry tomatoes. Bake for 45 mins until bubbling and golden.

Cheat's aubergine Parmigiana

Cook:55 mins - 1 hr and 2 mins **Serves 2**

Ingredients

- 2 medium aubergines
- 400g can chopped tomatoes
- 2 x 125g balls buffalo mozzarella
- 30g grated parmesan (or vegetarian alternative)

Method

STEP 1

Heat oven to 200C/180C fan/gas 6. Put the aubergines on a baking tray and make a slit down the centre of each. Drizzle with 2 tbsp olive oil and season. Bake for 50-55 mins or until the flesh is soft. Heat the grill. Tip the tomatoes into a bowl and season well. Fill the aubergines with layers of tomatoes and mozzarella, and finish with the Parmesan. Put under the grill for 5-7 mins until the cheese is golden.

Beef in barolo

Prep:10 mins **Cook:**4 hrs and 30 mins Plus chilling

Serves 4

Ingredients

- 4 small short ribs
- 750ml bottle barolo (or another full-bodied Italian red wine)
- 1 rosemary sprig
- 1 thyme sprig
- 5 sage leaves
- 1 bay leaf
- 1 tsp black peppercorns
- 1 tsp juniper berries
- 2 tbsp vegetable oil
- 250ml chicken stock

- 2 large onions , quartered
- 2 large carrots , cut into long wedges
- soft polenta with a drizzle of truffle oil, to serve

Method

STEP 1

The night before, put the beef in a large bowl. Pour over the wine, add the herbs, peppercorns and juniper berries, and leave to soak overnight. The following day, remove the beef and pat dry, setting aside the wine and aromatics. (You can skip this step if you don't have time.)

STEP 2

Heat oven to 160C/140C fan/gas 3. Heat 1 tbsp of the vegetable oil in a large casserole. Add the beef, browning all over except for the bone side, then remove and set aside. Add the red wine, herbs, peppercorns and juniper berries. Boil for around 15 mins until reduced by half, then return the meat to the pan and add the stock. Return the mixture to the boil, then cover with a lid and cook in the oven for 2½ hrs.

STEP 3

Fry the onion and carrot in a frying pan over a high heat until golden brown, then set aside. Remove the stew from the oven and carefully lift out the meat. Sieve the remaining pan contents into a large jug, discarding the contents of the sieve. The fat from the beef will rise to the surface – skim it off. Pour the skimmed sauce back into the casserole dish, then add the browned veg and meat. Cover, then return to the oven for another 1½ hrs, removing the lid for the last 30 mins to let the sauce reduce, then serve with polenta drizzled with truffle oil.

Quick & easy tiramisu

Prep:15 mins plus 1 hr chilling, No cook

Serves 2

Ingredients

- 3 tsp instant coffee granules
- 3 tbsp coffee liqueur (or Camp Chicory & Coffee Essence)
- 250g tub mascarpone
- 85g condensed milk

- 1 tsp vanilla extract
- 4-6 sponge fingers
- 1 tbsp cocoa powder

Method

STEP 1

Mix the coffee granules with 2 tbsp boiling water in a large jug and stir to combine. Add the coffee liqueur and 75ml cold water. Pour into a shallow dish and set aside.

STEP 2

Make the cream layer by beating the mascarpone, condensed milk and vanilla extract with an electric whisk until thick and smooth.

STEP 3

Break the sponge fingers into two or three pieces and soak in the coffee mixture for a few secs. Put a few bits of the sponge in the bottom of two wine or sundae glasses and top with the cream. Sift over the cocoa and chill for at least 1 hr before serving.

Ciabatta

Prep:30 mins **Cook:**40 mins plus resting and proving

makes 2 loaves

Ingredients

For the biga

- ¼ tsp dried active yeast
- 165g plain flour
- For the dough
- ½ tsp dried action yeast
- 35ml warm milk
- 1 tbsp olive oil

- 250g strong white bread flour

Method

STEP 1

The night before, make the biga (see tip, below). Stir yeast with 50ml warm water, stand for 10 mins, then add another 80ml warm water. Gradually add the flour in a stand mixer on its lowest setting. Once it's a wet dough, transfer to a well-oiled bowl, cover and leave for 12 hours or overnight at room temperature.

STEP 2

In the morning, combine the yeast and milk and leave to stand for 10 mins. Tip into a freestanding mixer fitted with a dough hook, add 160ml water, the biga and the olive oil. Then add the flour and 1 heaped tsp salt. Use the dough hook of a stand mixer to combine the dough. Knead for 10 mins until smooth and elastic. Don't worry if it looks very wet, it should to be a very wet dough! Pour into a well-oiled bowl and cover with cling film. Leave to prove for an hour and a half or until doubled in size.

STEP 3

Once rested, begin to do a series of folds – lift the dough from the edge, pull up, over, then release it. Turn the bowl 90 degrees and do the same again. Repeat so you do a full turn of the bowl twice, or 8 folds. Rest for 30 mins, then repeat the whole folding process once more.

STEP 4

Heat the oven to 220C/200C fan/gas mark 6. Tip the dough onto a really well-floured surface and cut in half. The dough will feel like a batter and spread across the surface a bit, but don't panic, just work on a well-floured surface, using the flour and a pastry scraper to help move the dough. Shape the dough into 2 large squares (about 20cm x 20cm). Dealing with each loaf at a time, fold the dough in from each side, as if folding a booklet. Flip over, then pick up the roll and place each onto separate well-floured sheets of baking paper. The roll will be very soft, so oil or flour your hands well. Allow to rest for another 30 mins, covered with a floured tea towel. Don't worry if it spreads a little.

STEP 5

While the dough rests, heat a baking sheet in the oven. Once the dough has rested, slide each of the loaves, along with the baking paper beneath them, onto the hot baking sheet. Bake for 35-40 mins, until the crust is golden and the loaves sound hollow when tapped on the base. Move to a wire rack and cool for an hour before slicing and serving with olive oil and balsamic vinegar.

Ricotta & spinach gnudi

Prep:40 mins **Cook:**4 hrs plus 1 hr 30 mins chilling, 4 mins cooking per batch

Serves 6

Ingredients

- 500g spinach, ends trimmed
- 500g ricotta (needs to be dry, so strain overnight if it's wet)
- 75g egg yolks
- 75g dried breadcrumbs
- 50g plain flour
- whole nutmeg, for grating
- 125g Grana Padano, grated, plus extra for the sauce and to serve
- 50g butter
- 20g sage, sliced if the leaves are large

Method

STEP 1

Pour boiling water over the spinach, then leave to cool a little before squeezing out any excess liquid. Chop the spinach finely. Drain and squeeze out any excess water again. Put the spinach in a mixing bowl with the ricotta, egg yolks, breadcrumbs, flour, a grating of nutmeg, a pinch of salt and the cheese. Mix well.

STEP 2

Scoop up 24 equal-sized lumps of the mixture, using an ice cream scoop if you have one, and shape each one into a log by rolling it between your hands. Lay each log on a baking sheet, then chill for 30 mins, or until needed.

STEP 3

Bring a large pan of salted water to the boil. Lower the gnudi into the water, turn down to a simmer and cook for 3-4 mins (do this in batches if you need to). Meanwhile, heat the butter in a large frying pan, add the sage and fry until crisp. Drain the gnudi well, then tip into the pan with the sage, along with a good grating of cheese. Swirl everything together, doing it in batches if it's easier. Arrange four gnudi on each serving plate, pour over more of the sauce and scatter with more grated cheese.

Roast sea bass & vegetable traybake

Prep: 10 mins **Cook:** 30 mins

Serves 2

Ingredients

- 300g red-skinned potatoes, thinly sliced into rounds
- 1 red pepper, cut into strips
- 2 tbsp extra virgin olive oil
- 1 rosemary sprig, leaves removed and very finely chopped
- 2 sea bass fillets
- 25g pitted black olive, halved
- ½ lemon, sliced thinly into rounds
- handful basil leaves

Method

STEP 1

Heat oven to 180C/160C fan/gas 4. Arrange the potato and pepper slices on a large non-stick baking tray. Drizzle over 1 tbsp oil and scatter with the rosemary, a pinch of salt and a good grinding of pepper. Toss everything together well and roast for 25 mins, turning over halfway through, until the potatoes are golden and crisp at the edges.

STEP 2

Arrange the fish fillets on top and scatter over the olives. Place a couple of lemon slices on top of the fish and drizzle with the remaining oil. Roast for further 7-8 mins until the fish is cooked through. Serve scattered with basil leaves.

Italian turkey steaks with garlicky bean mash

Prep: 10 mins **Cook:** 10 mins

Serves 4

Ingredients

- zest 2 lemons , juice from 1 ½
- 3 tbsp olive oil
- 3 garlic cloves , crushed
- 2 tsp chopped fresh oregano , or 1 tsp dried
- 4 thick turkey steaks
- 250g punnet cherry or small plum tomatoes , some halved, some left whole
- 750g bag frozen broad bean

Method

STEP 1

Heat oven to 200C/180C fan/gas 6 and bring a pan of water to the boil. Mix most of the lemon zest with the lemon juice, oil, garlic and seasoning. Set aside two-thirds, then mix the oregano into the rest. Pour this over the turkey steaks on a plate and turn them to coat.

STEP 2

Fry the turkey steaks in a non-stick frying pan for 1-2 mins on each side to brown, then transfer to a roasting tin. Scatter the tomatoes around, then roast in the oven for 4-8 mins, depending on the thickness of the turkey, until the steaks are just cooked through.

STEP 3

Meanwhile, cook the beans in the boiling water for 4-5 mins until tender. Tip a ladle of the cooking water into a food processor, then drain the beans and tip into the processor with the reserved lemon dressing. Whizz to a mash, then divide between 4 plates and top with a turkey steak, scattering over remaining lemon zest. Shake the tin so the tomatoes roll around in the cooking juices, then serve with the turkey.

Sgroppino

Prep:5 mins **Serves 1**

Ingredients

- 2 tsp lemon sorbet

- 1 tsp vodka
- champagne

Method

STEP 1

Put the lemon sorbet into the bottom of a champagne flute.

STEP 2

Pour over the vodka, then top with champagne.

Classic spaghetti Bolognese

Prep:10 mins **Cook:**1 hr

Serves 4

Ingredients

- 2 tbsp oil
- 1 large onion, finely chopped
- 2 celery sticks, finely chopped
- 2 carrots, finely chopped
- 50g pancetta cubes
- 400g lean beef mince
- 150g chicken livers, chopped, fat and sinew removed
- 1 large bay leaves
- 4 tbsp tomato purée
- 150ml white wine
- 500ml fresh chicken stock
- 300ml passata
- 500g pack spaghetti
- 50ml full-fat milk
- parmesan, grated, to serve

Method

STEP 1

Heat 1½ tbsp oil in a large pan or flameproof casserole dish over a low-medium heat. Add the onion, celery and carrots with a pinch of salt. Cook for 10 mins, stirring occasionally, until softened but not coloured. Transfer to a plate using a slotted spoon.

STEP 2

Pour the remaining oil into the pan, increase the heat and tip in the pancetta. Cook for 3-4 mins until golden. Add the mince and chicken livers, and cook for a further 5 mins until browned, breaking down the mince with the back of a wooden spoon.

STEP 3

Return the vegetables to the pan and add the bay leaf and tomato purée. Cook for a 1 min more and mix well. Pour in the wine and reduce by half. Add the stock and passata with some seasoning and bring to the boil. Reduce the heat to medium and let the sauce bubble away for 35-40 mins, stirring occasionally, until reduced by half and you are left with a thick ragu.

STEP 4

Bring a large saucepan of salted water to the boil 15 mins before the sauce is ready. Drop in the pasta, cook following pack instructions until al dente, then drain.

STEP 5

To finish the sauce, stir in the milk and season to taste. Tip the pasta onto a plate and top with the Bolognese. Serve with the Parmesan.

Best ever tiramisu

Prep:30 mins Plus chilling **Serves 6**

Ingredients

- 568ml pot double cream
- 250g tub mascarpone
- 75ml marsala
- 5 tbsp golden caster sugar
- 300ml strong coffee, made with 2 tbsp coffee granules and 300ml boiling water
- 175g pack sponge fingers
- 25g dark chocolate
- 2 tsp cocoa powder

Method

STEP 1

Put the double cream, mascarpone, marsala and golden caster sugar in a large bowl.

STEP 2

Whisk until the cream and mascarpone have completely combined and have the consistency of thickly whipped cream.

STEP 3

Pour the coffee into a shallow dish. Dip in a few of the sponge fingers at a time, turning for a few seconds until they are nicely soaked, but not soggy. Layer these in a dish until you've used half the sponge fingers, then spread over half of the creamy mixture.

STEP 4

Using the coarse side of the grater, grate over most of the dark chocolate. Then repeat the layers (you should use up all the coffee), finishing with the creamy layer.

STEP 5

Cover and chill for a few hours or overnight. Will keep in the fridge for up to two days.

STEP 6

To serve, dust with the cocoa powder and grate over the remainder of the chocolate.

Italian turkey toasties

Prep: 10 mins **Cook:** 10 mins

Ingredients

- 4 slices prosciutto
- 4 turkey breast steaks
- 4 tbsp pepperonata antipasto (such as Scala)
- 125g ball reduced-fat mozzarella , sliced into 8
- small bunch basil , leaves only
- medium ciabatta loaf, or 2 ciabatta rolls

- salad leaves , to serve

Method

STEP 1

Heat grill to high. Lay the prosciutto out on a large baking sheet and sit a turkey steak on top, crossways. Spread the turkey with the pepperonata, then top with 2 slices of mozzarella, a few basil leaves and some seasoning. Fold the ends of the prosciutto around the cheese to enclose. Grill for 10 mins until golden and cooked through. Leave to rest for 2 mins.

STEP 2

Cut the ciabatta into 4 or the rolls in half, then toast under the grill. Top with salad leaves, then sit the turkey on top and serve.

Pesto chicken stew with cheesy dumplings

Prep:50 mins **Cook:**2 hrs and 20 mins

Serves 8

Ingredients

- 2 tbsp olive oil
- 12-15 chicken thighs , skin removed, bone in
- 200g smoked bacon lardon or chopped bacon
- 1 large onion , chopped
- 4 celery sticks, chopped
- 3 leeks , chopped
- 4 tbsp plain flour
- 200ml white wine
- 1l chicken stock
- 2 bay leaves
- 200g frozen pea
- 140g sundried tomato
- 140g fresh pesto
- small bunch basil , chopped

For the dumplings

- 140g butter
- 250g self-raising flour
- 100g parmesan , grated
- 50g pine nut

Method

STEP 1

Heat the oil in a large casserole dish. Brown the chicken until golden on all sides – you might have to do this in batches – remove the chicken from the pan as you go and set aside.

STEP 2

Add the lardons to the pan and sizzle for a few mins, then add the onion, celery and leeks, and cook over a medium heat for 8-10 mins until the vegetables have softened. Stir in the flour, season and cook for a further 2 mins.

STEP 3

Gradually stir in the wine and allow it to bubble away, then stir in the stock. Return the chicken to the pan with the bay leaves and cover with a lid. Reduce the heat and simmer gently for 1½ hrs or until the chicken is tender. The stew can now be cooled and frozen if you're making ahead. Just defrost thoroughly, then gently warm through back in the pan before continuing.

STEP 4

Heat oven to 200C/180C fan/gas 6. Add the peas, sundried tomatoes, pesto and basil to the stew. To make the dumplings, rub the butter into the flour until it resembles fine breadcrumbs. Mix in the grated cheese and add 150ml water, mixing with a cutlery knife to bring the crumbs together to form a light and sticky dough. Break off walnut-sized lumps and shape into small balls. Roll the tops of the dumplings in the pine nuts so a few stick to the outside, then place the dumplings on top of the stew and scatter with any remaining nuts. Put the dish in the oven and bake for 25 mins until the dumplings are golden brown and cooked through. Serve with mashed potato and extra veg if you like.

Low-fat turkey bolognese

Prep:10 mins **Cook:**45 mins

Serves 4 - 6

Ingredients

- 400g lean turkey mince (choose breast instead of thigh mince if you can, as it has less fat)
- 2 tsp vegetable oil
- 1 large onion, chopped
- 1 large carrot, chopped
- 3 celery sticks, chopped
- 250g pack brown mushroom, finely chopped
- pinch of sugar
- 1 tbsp tomato purée
- 2 x 400g cans chopped tomato with garlic & herbs
- 400ml chicken stock, made from 1 low-sodium stock cube
- cooked wholemeal pasta and fresh basil leaves (optional), to serve

Method

STEP 1

Heat a large non-stick frying pan and dry-fry the turkey mince until browned. Tip onto a plate and set aside.

STEP 2

Add the oil and gently cook the onion, carrot and celery until softened, about 10 mins (add a splash of water if it starts to stick). Add the mushrooms and cook for a few mins, then add the sugar and tomato purée, and cook for 1 min more, stirring to stop it from sticking.

STEP 3

Add the tomatoes, turkey and stock with some seasoning. Simmer for at least 20 mins (or longer) until thickened. Serve with the pasta and fresh basil, if you have it.

Focaccia with pesto & mozzarella

Prep:20 mins - 25 mins **Cook:**30 mins Plus rising and proving

Serves 4 - 6

Ingredients

- 500g strong white bread flour, plus some for dusting

- 1 ½ tsp salt
- 7g sachet fast-action yeast
- 2 tbsp extra-virgin olive oil , plus some for drizzling
- 125g ball mozzarella , drained
- 5 tbsp pesto (shop-bought or see recipe, below)
- sea salt , to serve (optional)

Method

STEP 1

Put the flour into a bowl and mix in the salt. Mix the yeast into 325ml tepid water. Add the water and oil to the flour, then mix well with a plastic scraper or your hands. When most of the liquid is incorporated, use your hands to bring all the ingredients together into a ball of dough.

STEP 2

Tip the dough out onto a worktop lightly dusted with flour and work it by pulling and stretching for at least 10 mins. Try to get as much air into it as possible. Put the ball of worked dough into a well-oiled bowl, cover with a little more oil and a tea towel or cling film. Leave to rest for 1 hr or so in a non-draughty warm spot, until doubled in size.

STEP 3

Now stretch the dough out onto a baking sheet until it's about 20 x 30cm. Leave the dough to rise again to about half as high again, about 30-40 mins in a warm draught-free place, loosely covered with a tea towel.

STEP 4

Heat oven to 180C/160C fan/gas 4. When the dough has risen, press your fingers into it gently to make some holes. Bake for about 15 mins, then remove from the oven. Tear over the mozzarella, then bake for another 5-10 mins until golden and cooked through. Drizzle over the pesto and scatter with sea salt, if you like. Serve straight away.

Sherry, almond & orange pandoro

Prep:10 mins **Cook:**5 mins

Serves 12 - 15

Ingredients

- 300ml double cream
- 250g mascarpone
- 4 tbsp Pedro Ximénez sherry
- 1 large orange , zested
- 2 tbsp icing sugar , plus extra for dusting
- 1 pandoro
- 50g almonds , toasted and roughly chopped
- edible gold leaf (optional)

Method

STEP 1

In a large bowl, whisk together the cream, mascarpone, half the sherry, 3/ 4 of the zest and the icing sugar until the mixture is floppy and just holds its shape.

STEP 2

Cut the pandoro horizontally into five slices. Put the bottom piece on a serving plate or cake stand and drizzle over a little of the remaining sherry. Spoon over a quarter of the cream mixture and top with a handful of the almonds (saving enough for each layer and to decorate the top). Add the next layer of pandoro and continue to sandwich the layers together, rotating each at a different angle so that you create the shape of a Christmas tree.

STEP 3

Dust with icing sugar, then dot over the gold leaf (if using) along with the remaining almonds and orange zest.

Squash, pea & feta frittatinis

Prep:20 mins **Cook:**25 mins plus cooling

Makes 8

Ingredients

- 250g butternut squash , peeled, deseeded and chopped into small pieces
- 25g frozen peas

- 100g feta , crumbled
- 4 large eggs

Method

STEP 1

Heat oven to 200C/180C fan/gas 6. Put the butternut squash in a bowl, cover with cling film and cook in the microwave on High for 5-7 mins until tender. Meanwhile, line 8 holes of a muffin tin with squares of baking parchment – allow a little overhang at the top as the frittatinis will puff up.

STEP 2

Divide the squash, peas and feta between the lined muffin holes – they should be quite full. Beat the eggs in a jug with some seasoning, then pour into the muffin holes. Put the tin in the centre of the oven and bake for 20 mins. Leave to cool for about 15 mins before packing into a cooler bag for transporting, or chill for up to 24 hrs.

Walnut & red pepper pesto pasta

Prep:15 mins **Cook:**15 mins

Serves 4

Ingredients

- 400g strozzapreti or casarecce pasta , or another short pasta shape
- 100g walnut
- 3 roasted red peppers , roughly chopped
- 25g parmesan , or a vegetarian alternative, plus extra to serve
- 1 small garlic clove , roughly chopped
- large pack basil , plus a few leaves to serve
- 2 tbsp extra virgin olive oil
- 50g mascarpone

Method

STEP 1

Cook the pasta following pack instructions. Meanwhile, toast the walnuts in a dry pan for a few mins. Add half the walnuts to the small bowl of a food processor or a hand chopper, along with the red peppers, Parmesan, garlic, basil, oil and some seasoning. Whizz to a paste, adding a splash of water from the pasta if it is a little dry.

STEP 2

Drain the pasta, reserving a cup of the cooking water. Return the pasta to the pan and set over a low heat. Add the pesto, mascarpone and 3-4 tbsp of the reserved pasta water, then stir until the mascarpone has melted, adding a splash more pasta water if the sauce needs thinning. To serve, crush the remaining walnuts in your hand and scatter over the pasta with a few more basil leaves and some extra Parmesan.

Cannoli

Prep:40 mins **Cook:**30 mins plus resting and cooling

Makes 12

Ingredients

- 150g plain flour
- 1 tbsp golden caster sugar
- large pinch bicarbonate of soda
- ½ tsp cinnamon
- 1 tsp cocoa powder (optional)
- 30g butter
- 1 egg, separated
- 50ml dry marsala or white wine
- rapeseed oil or sunflower oil for deep-frying (see tip)
- 50g dark chocolate, melted
- handful pistachio kernels, finely chopped
- icing sugar, to dust

For the filling

- 250g ricotta, drained and beaten until fluffy
- 100g mascarpone
- 2 tbsp finely chopped candied peel

- 2 tbsp icing sugar

You will also need

- cannoli moulds (available to buy online)

Method

STEP 1

Tip the flour, sugar, bicarb, cinnamon and cocoa (if using) into a bowl with a pinch of salt. Add the butter and rub it into the dry ingredients until there are no more lumps. Mix the egg yolk and marsala and add this to the bowl, then mix the whole lot together and knead to a smooth dough. Wrap and rest in the fridge. (Can be made ahead and fried the next day.)

STEP 2

Fill a deep-fat fryer, wok or deep saucepan a third of the way up with oil. Cut the dough into pieces and, working one piece at a time, roll them out as thinly as you can – use a pasta machine if you have one. Heat the oil and keep an eye on it until it reaches 180C. Lay the dough out on a lightly floured surface and cut out circles about 11cm across. Wrap each one around a cannoli mould, using some of the egg white to stick the top edge down and they're ready for frying.

It's important to take care when cooking with hot oil. Read our guide on how to deep-fry safely to avoid accidents in the kitchen.

STEP 3

Deep-fry the cannoli (with their moulds) one at a time, making sure they cook all over. They should take about 45-60 seconds in all and should be visibly golden brown (keep cooking a little longer if they aren't) and the dough will bubble and blister. Carefully take each one out of the oil using the tongs and shake the cannoli off the mould very carefully onto kitchen paper. As you fry each one, make sure the oil stays at 180C at all times and doesn't get any hotter. These will keep for 2-3 days in an airtight container.

STEP 4

When the cannoli are cold, dip the end of each one into chocolate, then dip some of those into the pistachios. Leave to cool and harden. Beat the ricotta and mascarpone together, then stir in the candied peel and sugar. Spoon the mixture into a piping bag with a wide star nozzle and pipe it into the cannoli. Serve soon after filling.

Pumpkin, fennel & Taleggio galette

Prep: 35 mins **Cook:** 1 hr and 30 mins

Serves 6

Ingredients

- 700g pumpkin or 1 small squash
- 5 tbsp olive oil
- grating of nutmeg
- 2 small fennel bulbs
- juice ½ small lemon
- ½ tsp fennel seeds , toasted and coarsely crushed
- 470g spinach , coarse stalks removed
- 15g unsalted butter
- 1 garlic clove , crushed
- 1 egg yolk mixed with 2 tsp milk (to make an egg wash)
- 200g Taleggio (or vegetarian alternative), sliced
- 375g puff pastry

Method

STEP 1

Heat oven to 190C/170C fan/gas 5. Peel the squash, then halve and deseed it before cutting the flesh into thick wedges and halving them again to make quarters. Put the slices in a roasting tin with half the olive oil, the nutmeg and seasoning, and toss to coat. Roast for 30 mins, or until tender and a little caramelised.

STEP 2

Halve the fennel bulbs lengthways and remove the tops and tough outer leaves from each piece. Trim the base and cut each half into thick wedges, keeping them intact at the base. Put the wedges straight into a bowl and toss with the lemon juice to prevent discolouring. Add the fennel seeds, remaining olive oil and some seasoning, then toss well. Spread the fennel in a roasting tin large enough to hold it in a single layer and cover with foil. Roast the fennel (at the same time as the squash) for 20 mins, or until tender with pale -gold undersides.

STEP 3

Wash the spinach and cook in a covered pan over a medium heat for 1-2 mins. When wilted, drain in a colander and leave to cool. Squeeze the excess moisture out of the spinach, chop roughly and season. Melt the butter in a frying pan and quickly fry the spinach with the garlic for 3 mins. Set aside.

STEP 4

Roll out the pastry to make the base of the tart, ending up with a piece measuring roughly 28 x 38cm. Put the pastry base on to a floured metal baking sheet. Create a border all the way round by lightly running a knife 2cm from the edge. Prick the rest of the pastry all over with a fork. Put a rectangle of baking parchment, the size of the inside of the border, over the pastry. Weight it down with baking beans. Knock up the sides of the pastry by holding a small knife at a right angle to the pastry and making small indentations to release the layers. This will give you a better rise. Paint the border with the egg wash.

STEP 5

Put the pastry in the preheated oven and cook for 25 mins, removing the beans and paper after 15 mins. Take the partially cooked tart base out of the oven and, if the centre has risen, gently flatten it with the back of a wooden spoon. Turn the oven up to 200C/180C fan/gas 6.

STEP 6

Spoon the spinach onto the pastry, then put the squash and fennel on top. Distribute the cheese over the top, too. Put the tart back into the oven and cook for a further 25 mins. The cheese should be golden in patches and the pastry should be cooked and golden, but not too dark.

Prosecco cake

Prep:30 mins **Cook:**45 mins - 50 mins

Serves 18

Ingredients

- 350g unsalted butter , plus a little for the tins
- 350g golden caster sugar
- 6 eggs
- 350g self-raising flour
- 100ml prosecco
- 100g raspberry jam

For the buttercream

- 300g unsalted butter , softened
- 600g icing sugar
- 100ml prosecco
- To decorate
- sprinkles , coloured sugar, mini meringues, Prosecco-flavoured sweets, popcorn and lollies

Method

STEP 1

Heat oven to 160C/140C fan/gas 3. Butter the inside of 2 deep, loose bottomed 21cm tins. Cream the butter and sugar together with electric beaters until it is light and fluffy, then gradually beat in the eggs a little at a time. Fold in the flour and a pinch of salt, don't worry if the mixture look like it has split, it will come back together when the flour is added. Pour in the Prosecco and stir until smooth.

STEP 2

Spoon the mixture into the tins, level the top and bake for 45-50 mins or until the cakes are well-risen and golden and a skewer inserted comes out clean. Leave to cool in the tin for 10 minutes and then turn them out onto a rack.

STEP 3

While the cakes cool, make the icing. Beat the butter with the icing sugar until it is smooth. Add the Prosecco and beat again until the frosting is fluffy and smooth.

STEP 4

Level the cakes if you need to and spread the raspberry jam on one of the cakes followed by some of the butter cream, sandwich the other cake on top. Roughly ice the cake all over in a very thin layer with a couple of tablespoons of buttercream, this will help all the crumbs stick to the cake and help make the outer layer of icing nice and clean. Ice the cake all over with the remaining buttercream, this can be quite rough because you are going to stick sweet all over it. Now stick sweets all over it. Go mad. Drink Prosecco with it.

Strawberry panna cotta

Prep:30 mins **Cook:**25 mins plus cooling and 3 hrs chilling

Serves 6

Ingredients

For the panna cotta

- 3 gelatine leaves
- 450ml double cream
- 200ml whole milk
- 100g white caster sugar
- 1 vanilla pod

For the strawberries

- 400g strawberry , hulled and halved, or quartered if very large
- 1 ½ tsp cornflour
- 50g white caster sugar

Method

STEP 1

For the panna cotta, put the gelatine leaves in a small bowl of cold water to soften – this will take about 5 mins. Meanwhile, pour the cream, milk and sugar into a pan, split the vanilla pod, scrape out the seeds and add, along with the pod, to the cream mixture. Heat gently until hot, but not bubbling. Remove the gelatine leaves from the water, squeeze out any excess liquid then add, one at a time, to the hot cream. Stir until dissolved. Leave to stand for 20-30 mins until cooled – the vanilla pods should be suspended in the liquid by this point. Strain the mixture through a sieve into 6 serving glasses, then chill for at least 3 hrs.

STEP 2

Toss the strawberries with the cornflour and sugar in a saucepan. Place over a medium heat and cook for 4-5 mins, until the released juices thicken and the strawberries soften. Set aside to cool. Once completely cooled, top the set panna cottas with the strawberry mixture. Chill until ready to serve.

Beefy melanzane parmigiana

Prep:20 mins **Cook:**1 hr and 50 mins

Serves 6

Ingredients

- 2 tbsp olive oil , plus extra for brushing
- 800g beef mince
- 3 garlic cloves , crushed
- 3 thyme sprigs
- 3 rosemary sprigs
- 3 bay leaves
- 2 x 400g cans chopped tomato
- glass of red wine
- 1 beef stock cube
- 1 tbsp sugar
- 5 aubergines , sliced lengthways into 5mm slices
- 2 x 125g balls mozzarella , torn into small chunks
- 50g parmesan , grated
- 250g tub mascarpone

Method

STEP 1

Heat the oil in a large frying pan or flameproof casserole dish. Add the mince and brown over a high heat, breaking up with a wooden spoon as you go. (You may need to do this in batches.) Once well browned, tip onto a plate.

STEP 2

Add the remaining oil, the garlic and herbs to the pan and gently cook for 1 min. Tip in the tomatoes and red wine, and bring to a simmer, stirring up any meaty bits stuck to the bottom of the pan. Return the mince to the pan, crumble in the stock cube, and add sugar and seasoning. Gently simmer for at least 1 hr, stirring occasionally, splashing in more water to keep it saucy if you need to. If you have time to simmer for longer, go for it – the longer the better. Fish out the herb stalks and bay leaves.

STEP 3

Meanwhile, heat a griddle or frying pan. Brush the aubergine slices on both sides with olive oil, then griddle in batches. You want each slice softened and slightly charred, so don't have the heat too high or the aubergine will char before softening. Remove to a plate as you go.

STEP 4

Heat oven to 180C/160C fan/gas 4. Set aside some of each cheese to go on the top. In a large baking dish spread a spoonful of mince sauce over the base then top with a layer of aubergines and season well. Spoon over some more mince sauce, then scatter over some mozzarella, Parmesan and blobs of mascarpone. Add another layer of aubergines and some seasoning. Repeat, layering everything up and finish with a layer of meat sauce. Top with your reserved cheese and bake for 30-40 mins until the top is crisp and golden and mince bubbling.

Seared steak with celery & pepper caponata

Prep:10 mins **Cook:**30 mins

Serves 2

Ingredients

- 200g extra-lean fillet steak
- 140g fresh spinach
- For the caponata
- 1-cal oil spray
- 1 red onion , halved and sliced
- 2 garlic cloves , cut into slivers
- 400g can chopped tomato
- 2 celery sticks, sliced
- 1 orange pepper , deseeded, quartered and sliced
- 25g pitted black kalamata olive , halved (about 8)
- 1 tbsp caper
- ½ tsp dried oregano or 1 tbsp fresh
- 1 tsp balsamic vinegar

Method

STEP 1

For the caponata, spray a large, wide non-stick pan with 3 sprays of oil, and add the onion and garlic. Cover and cook for 5 mins, stirring halfway through to brown them.

STEP 2

Tip in the tomatoes and a can of water, then stir in all the other caponata ingredients. Cover the pan and leave to simmer for 30 mins.

STEP 3

Heat a griddle or small non-stick frying pan. Generously grind black pepper over the steak and sear on both sides, about 6 mins in total, until cooked to your liking. Allow to rest while you wilt the spinach in a covered pan on a low heat.

STEP 4

Spoon the caponata onto 2 serving plates, top with the spinach, then slice the beef and arrange on top.

Sausage sandwich with pesto

Prep:5 mins **Cook:**10 mins

Serves 1

Ingredients

- 2 herby Cumberland sausages , sliced in half lengthways
- 1 ciabatta roll , sliced in half
- 2 tbsp fresh pesto
- 1 roasted red pepper from a jar, sliced in half
- ½ x 125g ball mozzarella , sliced
- handful rocket

Method

STEP 1

Heat grill to high. Put the sausages on a baking sheet, cut-side down, and grill for 5-6 mins or until cooked through, then set aside. Lay the ciabatta roll halves, cut-side up, on a baking tray and spread each with pesto. Top each half with a pepper and mozzarella slice, then grill for 2 mins or until golden and bubbling. Add the sausages and a handful of rocket, and put the roll back together, pressing down firmly to hold the fillings in place.

Aubergine rolls with spinach & ricotta

Prep:15 mins **Cook:**45 mins

Serves 4

Ingredients

- 2 aubergines , cut into thin slices lengthways
- 2 tbsp olive oil
- 500g spinach
- 250g tub ricotta
- grating of nutmeg
- 350g jar tomato sauce
- 4 tbsp fresh breadcrumb
- 4 tbsp parmesan (or vegetarian alternative)

Method

STEP 1

Heat oven to 220C/200C fan/gas 7. Brush both sides of the aubergine slices with oil, then lay on a large baking sheet. Bake for 15-20 mins until tender, turning once.

STEP 2

Meanwhile, put the spinach in a large colander and pour over a kettle of boiling water to wilt. Cool, then squeeze out the excess water, so that it is dry. Mix with the ricotta, nutmeg and plenty of seasoning.

STEP 3

Dollop a spoonful of the cheesy spinach mix in the centre of each aubergine slice, fold over to make a parcel and lay, sealed-side down, in an ovenproof dish. Pour over tomato sauce, sprinkle with breadcrumbs and cheese, and bake for 20-25 mins until golden and piping hot.

Mushroom, ricotta & rocket tart

Prep:10 mins **Cook:**25 mins

Serves 4

Ingredients

- 1 sheet ready-rolled puff pastry
- 2 tbsp olive oil
- 525g family pack mushroom , halved or quartered if large
- 2 garlic cloves , 1 finely sliced, 1 crushed
- 250g tub ricotta
- good grating of nutmeg
- ¼ small pack parsley , leaves only, roughly chopped
- 50g rocket

Method

STEP 1

Heat oven to 220C/200C fan/gas 7 and place a baking sheet inside. Unroll the pastry onto a piece of baking parchment and score a border around the pastry about 1.5cm in from the edge. Place the pastry (still on the parchment) on the baking sheet and cook for 10-15 mins.

STEP 2

While the pastry bakes, heat the oil in a large lidded pan and cook the mushrooms for 2-3 mins, with the lid on, stirring occasionally. Remove the lid and add the sliced garlic, then cook for 1 min more to get rid of excess liquid.

STEP 3

Mix the crushed garlic with the ricotta and nutmeg, then season well. Remove the pastry from the oven and carefully push down the risen centre. Spread over the ricotta mixture, then spoon on the mushrooms and garlic. Bake for 5 mins, then scatter over the parsley and rocket.

Raspberry & lemon polenta cake

Prep:15 mins **Cook:**30 mins

Serves 8

Ingredients

For the cake

- 225g very soft butter
- 225g caster sugar , plus 1 tbsp
- 4 eggs , beaten
- 175g fine polenta
- 50g plain flour
- 1½ tsp baking powder
- ½ tsp vanilla extract
- finely grated zest of 1½ lemons
- 200g frozen raspberry , left frozen
- icing sugar , or more to taste (optional)

For the filling

- 100g soft cheese at room temperature (we used Philadelphia)
- 1 tbsp icing sugar , or more to taste
- finely grated zest of ½ lemon , plus a squeeze of juice
- 142ml tub double cream
- 100g frozen raspberry , defrosted

Method

STEP 1

Heat oven to 190C/fan 170C/gas 5 and butter two 20cm sandwich tins. Line the bottom of the tins with baking paper. In a large bowl, beat the butter and 225g caster sugar together until creamy and light. Gradually add the egg, little by little, until all the egg is worked in and the mix is pale and fluffy. If the mix looks like it's starting to split, add 1 tsp of the flour, then carry on.

STEP 2

Put the polenta in another bowl, then stir in the flour and baking powder. Beat the vanilla extract and zest into the eggy mix, then fold in the dry ingredients. Spoon half the batter into each tin and level the top. Scatter all but a handful of the raspberries over the mix and poke in gently. Sprinkle one of the sponges with the 1 tbsp sugar. Bake for 20 mins until risen and golden, but still with a little wobble under the crust.

STEP 3

Open the oven, whip out the sugar-crusted sponge and quickly poke the remaining frozen raspberries into the top. Bake both sponges for 10 more mins or until springy in the middle. If this sounds too tricky, just leave the sponges to bake for 30 mins – the cake won't look as glam, but will still taste great (you can add the leftover berries to the filling instead). Cool in the tin for 10 mins, then cool completely on a rack. Be careful when turning out the raspberry-topped sponge and slide it off its base rather than turning it upside down.

STEP 4

When the sponges are cold, beat the soft cheese with the icing sugar, lemon zest and a little of the juice to loosen if it needs it. Very lightly whip the cream so that it just holds its shape, then fold into the cheese. Fold in the defrosted raspberries. Use to sandwich the sponges together, sugar-crusted on top, and serve dusted with more icing sugar.

Pizza dough

Prep:15 mins plus rising (no cook)

Makes 4 pizzas

Ingredients

- 500g '00' flour or plain flour, plus extra for dusting
- 1 tsp salt
- ½ tsp dried yeast (not fast-action)
- 400ml warm water
- oil, for greasing

Method

STEP 1

It's easiest to make this in a standing mixer with a dough hook (otherwise mix it in a bowl and knead on your work surface). Put the flour and salt in the bowl and mix the yeast into the water. It's always a good idea to wait 5 mins before using the liquid to see if the yeast is working – little bits will start to rise to the top and you'll know it's active.

STEP 2

Turn on the motor and pour in the liquid. Keep the speed on medium-high and it should come together as a ball. If the bottom is still sticking, tip in 1-2 tbsp of flour. Knead for 5-7 mins until the dough is shiny and it springs back when you press your finger into it. (If kneading by hand, it will take you about 10 mins.) Try not to add too much flour if you can. This is a slightly sticky dough, but that keeps it light and it rises beautifully.

STEP 3

Use oiled hands to remove the dough from the hook and bowl. Oil another bowl and place the dough in it. Turn it around so that it's lightly coated in the oil. Cover tightly with cling film and then a tea towel. Place in a draught-free area that's warm and leave until the dough has doubled in size. If it's a hot day, it should only take 2 hrs to rise, but it could take 4 hrs if it's cold. (If you don't plan to use the dough for a day or two, place it in the fridge straight away; take it out 3-4 hrs before using. Punch it down first and bring it together on a floured surface.)

STEP 4

Divide the dough into 2 pieces for big pizzas or 4 for plate-sized ones, then shape into balls (see Shaping the dough in tips, below) – dust them in flour as they will be sticky. Keep them covered with a tea towel or cling film while you prepare the toppings. (you can also freeze them in sealed bags. Just thaw in the fridge on the day, then bring to room temperature 3 hrs before using.)

STEP 5

To shape the dough: If you want to get air pockets and a light but crisp dough, then don't use a rolling pin. It flattens and pops the air bubbles. (Two days in the fridge will produce the most air bubbles – take it out three to four hours before using.) If your dough is at room temperature, you can use your fingers to gently stretch the dough out. Once it's about 16cm, place the disc over the tops of your hands (not palm side) and use them to stretch it further, up to about 25cm. You can start pressing out the other discs, then wait to do the final bit when you're ready to cook. Once you've mastered stretching the dough out, you can experiment with other shapes: rectangles, rounds or squares all look authentic.

STEP 6

To cook the pizza: An outdoor gas barbecue is best for controlling the temperature, but charcoal will give your pizza a more authentic, smoky flavour. For gas, turn the flames down to medium-low so that the bottom of the pizza doesn't burn. When cooking on a charcoal barbecue, let the coals turn grey before you pop on the pizza.

STEP 7

Place the pizza on a floured baking sheet (with no edge) or a pizza peel – this is a flat pizza paddle with a long handle, which makes it easier to get the dough on and off the grill. The flour will provide the 'wheels' for it to slide onto the grill – don't use oil as it sticks more and won't transfer as well.

STEP 8

Make sure the grill is hot and the flames have died back if cooking on charcoal. Slide the dough onto the grill, close the lid (if your barbecue has one) and give it three to four minutes. The dough will puff up; it's ready when the bottom has light brown stripes. Use tongs to pull the dough off and turn it upside down.

STEP 9

Assemble the pizza of your choice – see 'Goes well with', right, for topping suggestions. Remember that less is more, as the dough will stay crisper and the toppings will cook better.

STEP 10

Place the pizza back on the grill, uncooked-side down, and shut the lid. Give it another three to four minutes, then remove when the cheese is melted and the toppings are hot.

Roasted tomato, basil & Parmesan quiche

Prep:40 mins **Cook:**40 mins

Serves 8

Ingredients

- 300g cherry tomato
- drizzle olive oil
- 50g parmesan (or vegetarian alternative), grated
- 2 eggs
- 284ml pot double cream
- handful basil leaves, shredded, plus a few small ones left whole for scattering

For the pastry

- 280g plain flour, plus extra for dusting
- 140g cold butter, cut into pieces

Method

STEP 1

To make the pastry, tip the flour and butter into a bowl, then rub together with your fingertips until completely mixed and crumbly. Add 8 tbsp cold water, then bring everything together with your hands until just combined. Roll into a ball and use straight away or chill for up to 2 days. The pastry can also be frozen for up to a month.

STEP 2

Roll out the pastry on a lightly floured surface to a round about 5cm larger than a 25cm tin. Use your rolling pin to lift it up, then drape over the tart case so there is an overhang of pastry on the sides. Using a small ball of pastry scraps, push the pastry into the corners of the tin. Chill in the fridge or freezer for 20 mins. Heat oven to 200C/fan 180C/gas 6.

STEP 3

In a small roasting tin, drizzle the tomatoes with olive oil and season with salt and pepper. Put the tomatoes in a low shelf of the oven.

STEP 4

Lightly prick the base of the tart with a fork, line the tart case with a large circle of greaseproof paper or foil, then fill with baking beans. Blind-bake the tart for 20 mins, remove the paper and beans, then continue to cook for 5-10 mins until biscuit brown.

STEP 5

When you remove the tart case from the oven, take out the tomatoes, too.

STEP 6

While the tart is cooking, beat the eggs in a large bowl. Gradually add the cream, then stir in the basil and season. When the case is ready, sprinkle half the cheese over the base, scatter over the tomatoes, pour over the cream mix, then finally scatter over the rest of the cheese. Bake for 20-25 mins until set and golden brown. Leave to cool in the case, trim the edges of the pastry, then remove from the tin. Scatter over the remaining basil and serve in slices.

Rosemary chicken with tomato sauce

Prep:5 mins **Cook:**30 mins

Serves 4

Ingredients

- 1 tbsp olive oil
- 8 boneless, skinless chicken thighs
- 1 rosemary sprig, leaves finely chopped
- 1 red onion, finely sliced
- 3 garlic cloves, sliced
- 2 anchovy fillets, chopped
- 400g can chopped tomatoes
- 1 tbsp capers, drained
- 75ml red wine (optional)

Method

STEP 1

Heat half the oil in a non-stick pan, then brown the chicken all over. Add half the chopped rosemary, stir to coat, then set aside on a plate.

STEP 2

In the same pan, heat the rest of the oil, then gently cook the onion for about 5 mins until soft. Add the garlic, anchovies and remaining rosemary, then fry for a few mins more until fragrant. Pour in the tomatoes and capers with the wine, if using, or 75ml water if not. Bring to the boil, then return the chicken pieces to the pan. Cover, then cook for 20 mins until the chicken is cooked through. Season and serve with a crisp green salad and crusty bread.

Penne with chorizo & broccoli

Prep:5 mins **Cook:**20 mins

Serves 4

Ingredients

- 400g penne
- small head of broccoli , broken into small florets
- 200g cooking chorizo , diced
- 2 garlic cloves , crushed

- 1 tbsp fennel seed
- 200g low-fat cream cheese with garlic & herbs
- parmesan and rocket leaves, to serve

Method

STEP 1

Cook the penne following pack instructions, adding the broccoli for the final 3 mins. When cooked, drain, reserving a splash of the cooking water.

STEP 2

Meanwhile, fry the chorizo in a large dry frying pan until it starts to turn golden and release its oils. Add the garlic and fennel seeds, and cook for 1 min more. When the penne is cooked, tip it into the pan with the chorizo. Add the cream cheese, stir together until melted, adding a splash of the reserved cooking water so the sauce coats the pasta.

STEP 3

Serve in bowls, scattered with a few rocket leaves and some grated Parmesan, if you like.

Rye pizza with figs, fennel, gorgonzola & hazelnuts

Prep:1 hr **Cook:**45 mins plus 2-3 hrs rising

makes 2 x 30cm pizzas

Ingredients

For the dough

- 5g active dried yeast
- 250g strong white flour
- 125g '00' flour
- 125g rye flour
- ½ tsp sugar
- 1 tsp olive oil
- semolina flour , for dusting

For the topping

- 1 large fennel bulb , any fronds reserved
- juice 1/2 small lemon
- 1 tbsp olive oil
- 2 medium onions , halved and very finely sliced
- ¼ tsp fennel seeds , coarsely crushed in a mortar
- a little extra virgin olive oil , for drizzling
- 12 small figs , halved
- 1 ½ tbsp balsamic vinegar
- a little caster sugar , for sprinkling
- 180g gorgonzola (or vegetarian alternative), broken into chunks
- 2 tbsp hazelnuts , halved and toasted

Method

STEP 1

To make the dough, mix the yeast in a small bowl with 2 tbsp warm water and 1 tbsp strong white flour. Leave somewhere warm to 'sponge' for 20 mins or so (this dissolves and activates the yeast). Tip the three flours into a large bowl and make a well in the centre. Pour in the sponged yeast, 1 tsp salt, sugar, oil and 290ml warm water, and mix to form a wet dough. Knead for 10 mins until satiny and elastic, then put in a clean bowl, cover with a cloth and leave to double in size for 2 1/2 - 3 hrs.

STEP 2

Quarter the fennel bulb lengthways and remove any tough outer leaves. Trim the base of each, thinly slice with a knife or mandolin, then put in a bowl with the lemon juice so it doesn't turn brown.

STEP 3

Heat the oil in a frying pan, add the onions and a pinch of salt, and fry over a medium heat for 7 mins. Add 1-2 tbsp of water, season with pepper, cover and cook on a low heat for 10 mins until softened. Add most of the fennel, along with the fennel seeds and seasoning, and cook for 3 mins, stirring every so often. If the mixture is still wet, uncover and bubble off any liquid.

STEP 4

An hour before cooking, heat the oven to its highest setting and put a baking sheet or pizza stone in to heat. Tip the dough onto a lightly floured surface, knead it a little, then halve and roll each piece into a circle or rough square. Lift the dough and, while rotating, stretch with your fingertips until each piece is 30-32cm across and as thin as possible with a slightly thicker edge.

STEP 5

Sprinkle two large baking sheets with semolina and put the pizza bases on them. Top each base with the cooked onion and fennel mix, then the pieces of raw fennel, leaving a 3cm border. Drizzle with a little olive oil. Put the halved figs on top and spoon on a little balsamic vinegar and a sprinkle of sugar. Grind over some pepper. Carefully slide the first pizza onto the heated baking sheet in the oven. Bake for 8-12 mins until the dough is golden and the figs caramelised. Halfway through the cooking time, dot the pizza with the cheese. Scatter on the toasted hazelnuts and any reserved fennel fronds. Repeat with the second pizza.

Bacon & mushroom risotto

Prep:10 mins **Cook:**30 mins

Serves 4

Ingredients

- 1 tbsp olive oil
- 1 onion, chopped
- 8 rashers streaky bacon, chopped
- 250g chestnut mushroom, sliced
- 300g risotto rice
- 1l hot chicken stock
- grated parmesan, to serve

Method

STEP 1

Heat the oil in a deep frying pan and cook the onion and bacon for 5 mins to soften. Add the mushrooms and cook for a further 5 mins until they start to release their juices. Stir in the rice and cook until all the juices have been absorbed.

STEP 2

Add the stock, a ladleful at a time, stirring well and waiting for most of the stock to be absorbed before adding the next ladleful – it will take about 20 mins for all the stock to be added. Once the rice is cooked, season and serve with the grated Parmesan.

Roast aubergine parmigiana

Prep:20 mins **Cook:**1 hr and 15 mins

Serves 4

Ingredients

- 2 tbsp extra-virgin olive oil
- 2 garlic cloves , crushed
- small bunch basil , stalks finely chopped
- 2 x 400g cans cherry tomatoes
- 1 tbsp chopped sundried or semi-dried tomato
- 1 tsp clear honey
- few thyme sprigs, leaves removed
- 4 medium aubergines
- 2 balls light mozzarella , thinly sliced
- 25g breadcrumb
- 25g parmesan (or vegetarian alternative), finely grated
- crusty bread , to serve (optional)

Method

STEP 1

Heat 1 tbsp of the oil in a pan. Soften the garlic and the basil stalks for 1 min, without letting the garlic colour. Add both types of tomatoes, the honey, most of the thyme leaves and plenty of seasoning. Simmer for 5 mins – you don't want the sauce to reduce too much at this stage.

STEP 2

Meanwhile, heat oven to 200C/180C fan/gas 6. Cut 6 slits down into the flesh of each aubergine crosswise, taking care not to cut all the way through. Season inside, then push a slice of the mozzarella and a basil leaf into each gap.

STEP 3

Pour the tomato sauce into a large baking dish and sit the aubergines in it (or use 4 individual dishes). Drizzle with the remaining oil. Cover with foil and scrunch it tightly at the edges. Bake for 50 mins-1 hr until soft.

STEP 4

Remove the foil. Mix the breadcrumbs and Parmesan, and scatter over the aubergines with the rest of the thyme. Bake, uncovered, for another 15 mins or until the aubergines are very tender and the crumbs are golden and crisp. (The best way to tell if they are ready is to prod the largest aubergine in the centre with a skewer.) Let the dish rest for 5 mins, then scatter over the rest of the basil leaves. Serve with crusty bread, if you like.

Spring chicken one-pot

Prep:10 mins **Cook:**55 mins

Serves 4

Ingredients

- 1 tbsp olive oil
- 8 chicken thighs , skin on and bone in
- 1 onion , sliced
- 200g streaky bacon , chopped
- 1 carrot , chopped
- 2 large spring greens , shredded
- 600ml chicken stock
- 300g baby new potato
- 2 tbsp crème fraîche
- 2 tbsp basil pesto
- crusty bread , to serve (optional)

Method

STEP 1

Heat the oil in a large, heavy-based pan with a lid. Season the chicken and brown all over. Remove the chicken to a plate and cook the onion and bacon for 5 mins until softened and lightly coloured.

STEP 2

Return the chicken to the pan, and add the remaining ingredients, except the crème fraîche and pesto, along with plenty of freshly ground black pepper. Bring to the boil, then cover and gently simmer for 30-40 mins until the potatoes are tender and chicken cooked through.

STEP 3

Stir in the crème fraîche and pesto. Serve with some crusty bread for mopping up the sauce, if you like.

Kale pesto

Prep:10 mins No cook

Makes enough for 10-12 servings

Ingredients

- 85g pine nut , toasted
- 85g parmesan (or vegetarian alternative), coarsely grated, plus extra to serve (optional)
- 3 garlic cloves
- 75ml extra-virgin olive oil , plus extra to serve
- 75ml olive oil
- 85g kale
- juice 1 lemon
- spaghetti or linguine, to serve

Method

STEP 1

Put the pine nuts, Parmesan, garlic, oils, kale and lemon juice in a food processor and whizz to a paste. Season to taste. Stir through hot pasta to serve, topping with extra Parmesan and olive oil, if you like.

STEP 2

To store, put in a container or jar, cover the surface with a little more olive oil and keep in the fridge for a week, or freeze for up to a month.

Lemon meringue cake

Prep:2 hrs **Cook:**1 hr

Serves 16

Ingredients

For the lemon curd

- 75g unsalted butter , softened
- 225g caster sugar
- zest 3 lemons
- 100ml lemon juice , sieved to remove any seeds and pith
- 3 large eggs
- 1 tbsp cornflour

For the caramel sugar syrup

- 85g caster sugar

For the cake

- 300g unsalted butter , softened
- 200g caster sugar
- 75g light muscovado sugar
- 300g self-raising flour
- 5 medium eggs , beaten
- 25g cornflour
- 1 tsp baking powder
- zest 4 lemons

For the caramelised lemon slices

- 1 lemon
- 175g caster sugar

For the Italian meringue

- 300g caster sugar
- 6 medium egg whites

- ½ tsp cream of tartar

Method

STEP 1

Start by making the curd. Put all the ingredients in a saucepan and whisk together. It will look like it has curdled but don't worry – simply put the pan over a low heat and stir constantly until it is smooth and thick enough to coat the back of a spoon. Pass the mixture through a sieve into a bowl. Leave to cool, covered with cling film. Put in the fridge until ready to use, preferably overnight.

STEP 2

For the caramel sugar syrup, heat the caster sugar in a saucepan over a medium heat until it melts and starts to caramelise. Stir until smooth and a deep golden colour. Remove from the heat and carefully pour in 50ml boiling water. It will steam and spit a little, so take care. (If the sugar hardens, pop the pan back on the heat for 1-2 mins to melt again.) Stir, pour immediately into a heatproof jug and top up with a little extra boiling water (about 10ml) so you have 100ml of liquid in total. Leave on one side to cool.

STEP 3

To make the cake, heat oven to 180C/160C fan/gas 4. Grease 3 x 20cm sandwich tins, lining the bases and sides with baking parchment.

STEP 4

In a large bowl, beat together the butter and sugars with an electric whisk until light and fluffy. Mix in 1 tbsp flour, then add the eggs, a little at a time, beating after each addition until fully combined.

STEP 5

Mix together the remaining dry ingredients, the lemon zest and 1/2 tsp salt, then fold in to the butter mixture with the caramel sugar syrup. Divide the batter between the tins and level the tops with the back of a wet spoon. Bake for 25-30 mins or until a skewer inserted into the middle comes out clean. Allow the cakes to cool in the tins for 10 mins, then turn out onto a wire rack, peeling off the parchment. Leave to cool completely.

STEP 6

Make the caramelised lemon slices while the cakes are baking. Slice the lemon into 5mm thick slices, discarding the ends. In a shallow non-stick pan, bring 350ml water and the sugar to the boil. Add the lemon slices, boil for 10 mins, then reduce the heat to a simmer for 20-25 mins until the liquid has evaporated and the slices have caramelised. Remove from the pan and put on a non-stick A silicone mat or baking parchment to cool.

STEP 7

To assemble the cake. Place a sponge the right way up on a cake board or presentation plate. Top with an even layer of curd but don't go right to the edge, leave about 1cm uncovered. Gently put the next sponge on top and repeat the process, putting the last sponge upside down on top.

STEP 8

To make the Italian meringue, put the sugar and 175ml water in a saucepan and B bring to a rolling boil over a high heat. Continue to boil until it reaches 115C on a sugar thermometer. Meanwhile, put the egg whites and cream of tartar in a large mixing bowl (a tabletop mixer is ideal if you have one). Whisk the egg whites to soft peaks (when lifting the whisk out, the peaks should slowly vanish back into the mixture). Whisk the egg whites at high speed and very slowly trickle in the hot syrup. The meringue will C begin to thicken and go glossy after about 10 mins. Continue to whisk until it is still just warm. Use the meringue immediately, as it is easier to work with while warm.

STEP 9

Using a palette knife, spread a thin layer of meringue around the side of the cake to level and square it up, then spread an even layer about 3mm thick on the top of the cake (see step-by-step for guidance). Put the remaining meringue in a large piping bag fitted with a small star nozzle and pipe vertical columns up the side of the cake, level with the top. Finally, pipe small meringue stars on the top of the columns. It's easier to do this with the cake on a turntable.

STEP 10

Brown the meringue using a kitchen blowtorch. Finally, cut the caramelised lemon slices in half and use to decorate the top of the cake. Will keep for 3 days in the fridge.

Ravioli with artichokes, leek & lemon

Prep:10 mins **Cook:**10 mins

Serves 2

Ingredients

- 280g jar artichoke antipasto, drained reserving 1 tbsp oil, artichokes roughly chopped
- 1 large leek , finely sliced
- 1 garlic clove , crushed
- 3 tbsp cream cheese
- zest and juice 1 lemon
- 250g pack spinach & ricotta ravioli
- 2 large handfuls rocket and grated Parmesan (or vegetarian alternative) to serve (optional)

Method

STEP 1

Heat the oil from the artichokes in a large saucepan, then add the leek and garlic. Fry for 5 mins over a medium heat until the leek is soft. Stir in the artichokes, cream cheese and lemon zest, then heat through. Season to taste and add a squeeze of lemon juice.

STEP 2

Meanwhile, cook the ravioli following pack instructions. Drain, add to the pan with the artichokes and cream cheese, and toss through. Serve topped with the rocket and a grating of Parmesan, if you like.

Stuffed porchetta

Prep:30 mins **Cook:**3 hrs and 5 mins plus at least 8 hrs chilling, 1 hr standing and 30 mins resting

Serves 6 - 8

Ingredients

- 1 ½kg bone-out pork belly
- 1 tbsp bicarbonate of soda
- 3 tsp fennel seeds
- 1 tsp chilli flakes

For the stuffing

- 1 tbsp extra virgin olive oil
- 1 medium onion , finely chopped
- ½ fennel bulb , hard core cut out and discarded, the rest finely chopped
- ½ tsp coriander seeds , crushed
- 2 garlic cloves , crushed
- 250g minced pork shoulder
- 1 slice sourdough bread, torn into small pieces
- 25g toasted pine nuts
- grated zest 1 unwaxed orange
- 3 dried apricots , finely chopped
- 3 sage leaves , finely chopped
- ½ tbsp rosemary leaves, chopped
- ½ tbsp lemon juice
- freshly grated nutmeg
- 1 egg , beaten

Method

STEP 1

Score the pork belly skin with a sharp knife in a cross pattern. Score down to just before where the skin meets the fat, rather than the fat itself. Bring a large saucepan of water to a simmer and add the bicarbonate of soda. Lower the pork into the water, poach gently for 5 mins, then remove it from the water and leave to cool to room temperature.

STEP 2

Meanwhile, toast the fennel seeds and chilli flakes in a dry frying pan over a high heat for 1-2 mins, then tip into a bowl and leave to cool. Grind the spices in a spice grinder or with a pestle and mortar, then mix with 1 tbsp fine sea salt.

STEP 3

Once the pork has cooled, turn it skin-side down and pierce the underside of the meat all over with a knife. Rub the meat with the spiced salt rub, cover and put it in the fridge for at least 8 hrs or overnight. Can be prepared 24 hours ahead.

STEP 4

The next day, make your stuffing. Heat the olive oil in a non-stick frying pan and add the onion and fennel. Season and cook gently over a low heat for 10 mins. Add the coriander seeds and garlic, and cook for another 2 mins, then add the mince. Cook for 8-10 mins until the mince is browned. Set aside and leave to cool.

STEP 5

Transfer the mince and onion mix to a bowl and add the sourdough, pine nuts, orange zest, apricots, herbs, lemon juice and nutmeg. Season well, then mix together thoroughly with your hands. Add the egg and mix again.

STEP 6

Lie the pork belly on a board, skin-side down. Form the stuffing into a sausage shape running all the way down the middle of the belly. Wrap the sides of the belly around the stuffing and tie with butcher's string. Place seam-side down in a roasting tin, uncovered, and chill for at least 2 hrs, preferably overnight. You want the skin to dry out completely so that it crisps up when you roast it.

STEP 7

To cook the pork, remove it from the fridge and leave it for at least 1 hr to come to room temperature before you cook it. Heat oven to 180C/160C fan/ gas 4 and cook the pork for about 2 hrs, turning the tin every 30 mins or so. After 2 hrs, turn the heat up to 220C/ 200C fan/gas 7 and cook for another 20 mins. When the pork is done, a thermometer pushed into its centre should read 77C. If the skin looks in danger of burning, cover it with foil – but only do this once it has crackled.

STEP 8

Once the pork has cooked, remove from the oven and leave to rest for 30 mins. When you're ready to carve, put the pork on a big chopping board. Using a sharp knife, slice the meat into rounds.

Sea bream in crazy water (Orata all'acqua pazza)

Prep:10 mins **Cook:**30 mins

Serves 4

Ingredients

- 4 tbsp good quality extra-virgin olive oil
- 2 whole sea bream or sea bass (about 450g each), gutted and cleaned
- 2 garlic cloves , finely sliced
- ½ small red chilli , chopped
- 400g small tomato (a mix of different-coloured cherry tomatoes would be best)
- 4 tbsp white wine
- small handful capers
- chopped parsley

Method

STEP 1

Heat half the oil in a large, lidded frying pan. Carefully slip the fish into the sizzling oil and cook for 4-5 mins until starting to brown. Flip over and scatter the garlic around the fish. Sizzle for 1 min more, then add the chilli and scatter over the tomatoes. Pour over the wine and let it bubble for 1 min, then pour over 100ml water and season generously with sea salt and pepper.

STEP 2

Put on the lid, turn up the heat and simmer for 15 mins until the fish is cooked through – you can tell when the eyes turn bright white and the flesh feels softer.

STEP 3

Lift each fish out the pan onto a serving plate and put the pan back on the heat. Add the capers and parsley, and boil hard for 1 min. You can now serve the fish and the sauce separately or slip them back into the pan, spoon some of the sauce over and bring the pan to the table. Drizzle with a little more oil just before serving.

Creamy chicken & green bean pesto pasta

Prep:10 mins **Cook:**10 mins

Serves 4

Ingredients

- 400g pasta shapes

- 250g green bean, trimmed
- 1 tbsp olive oil
- 1 bunch spring onions, finely sliced
- 2 large ready-roasted chicken breasts, shredded
- 5 tbsp pesto
- 3 tbsp double cream
- handful parmesan, grated, to serve

Method

STEP 1

Cook pasta following pack instructions, adding green beans for the final 6 mins of cooking time. Drain and reserve a few tbsps of the cooking water.

STEP 2

Meanwhile, heat olive oil in a large frying pan. Add spring onions and cook for 1-2 mins until soft, then set aside.

STEP 3

Add the shredded chicken in the pan and heat through. Stir through pesto and cream. Pop pasta and beans in with the chicken mix and stir to coat, adding a little of the cooking water. Season and sprinkle with Parmesan.

Gnocchi with courgette, mascarpone & spring onions

Prep:5 mins **Cook:**15 mins

Serves 2

Ingredients

- 300g fresh gnocchi
- 1 tbsp olive oil
- 1 red chilli , sliced, deseeded if you like
- 1 medium courgette , cut into thin ribbons with a peeler
- 4 spring onions , chopped

- zest 1 lemon
- 2 heaped tbsp mascarpone
- 50g parmesan (or vegetarian alternative), grated
- dressed mixed leaves , to serve

Method

STEP 1

Cook the gnocchi following pack instructions. Drain, reserving a ladle of the cooking water, and set aside.

STEP 2

Heat the oil in a frying pan. Cook chilli and courgette for 3 mins until soft. Add spring onions, zest, mascarpone, half the Parmesan and cooking water. Mix until smooth, add gnocchi and heat through.

STEP 3

Season, divide between 2 ovenproof dishes and scatter with the remaining Parmesan. Grill for 2-3 mins until bubbling and serve with the dressed mixed leaves.

Pancake cannelloni

Prep:30 mins **Cook:**30 mins

Serves 4

Ingredients

- 420g pack free-range pork meatballs
- 400g bag fresh spinach
- 2 tbsp basil pesto
- 250g tub ricotta
- 1 egg , beaten
- ¼ tsp ground nutmeg
- 8 pre-made pancakes
- 500g carton passata
- 1 garlic clove , crushed
- 125g ball mozzarella , torn

- 1 bunch of basil , leaves only

Method

STEP 1

Heat the grill to high and cook the meatballs for 12-15 mins on a baking tray or following pack instructions. Cut each one in half and set aside.

STEP 2

Tip the spinach into a large colander over the sink. Pour boiling water over to wilt it and leave to drain thoroughly. When cool enough to handle, squeeze out any excess liquid and chop finely. Mix the spinach with the pesto, ricotta, egg and nutmeg, then season to taste.

STEP 3

Heat oven to 190C/170C fan/gas 5. Pour the passata over the bottom of an ovenproof dish and stir in the garlic. Divide the spinach mixture between the pancakes, spreading it out in a long strip in the centre. Add meatball pieces to each one, then roll the pancake up to seal in the filling. Lay the stuffed pancakes on the passata base and top with the mozzarella. Bake for 30 mins until the cheese is melted and bubbling. Scatter over basil leaves to serve.

Gnocchi with pancetta, spinach & Parmesan cream

Total time 15 mins **Serves 4**

Ingredients

- 500g pack gnocchi
- 1 garlic clove, sliced
- 1 tbsp olive oil
- 100ml double cream
- freshly grated nutmeg
- 130g pack smoked pancetta cubes
- 100g spinach
- zest ½ lemon
- 25g parmesan, grated, plus extra for serving
- 25g toasted pine nut

Method

STEP 1

Cook the gnocchi following pack instructions, then drain. Meanwhile, heat 1 tsp of the oil in a small pan and fry the garlic, then add the cream and a good grating of nutmeg. Put to one side.

STEP 2

Heat 2 tsp of the remaining oil in a frying pan and cook the pancetta until crisp. Add the gnocchi and fry until it starts to turn golden, adding a little more oil if it begins to stick. Stir in the spinach, lemon zest and seasoning.

STEP 3

Stir the Parmesan into the cream sauce. Spoon the gnocchi onto plates, drizzle over the sauce and scatter with pine nuts. Serve with extra Parmesan.

Orange polenta cake

Prep:20 mins **Cook:**45 mins

Serves 8 - 10

Ingredients

- 250g unsalted butter
- 250g golden caster sugar
- 4 large eggs
- 140g polenta
- 200g plain flour
- 2 tsp baking powder
- zest and juice 2 oranges (less 100ml juice for the glaze)

For the orange glaze

- 100ml orange juice
- 100g golden caster sugar

Method

STEP 1

Heat oven to 160C/140C fan/gas 3. Line the base and sides of a round 23cm cake tin with baking parchment. Cream the butter and sugar together until light and fluffy. Add the eggs one at a time and mix thoroughly. Once the mixture is combined, add all the dry ingredients and the zest and juice after you have measured off 100ml for the glaze.

STEP 2

Transfer the mixture to the tin, spread evenly, then cook for about 45 mins or until a skewer inserted into the centre of the cake comes out clean. Remove from the oven and turn out onto a wire rack to cool.

STEP 3

To make the glaze, put the juice and sugar in a medium saucepan and bring to the boil. Let it simmer for 5 mins, then remove from the heat and allow to cool. Drizzle the orange glaze over the top of the cooled cake. Serve with Lemon ice cream, below.

Orecchiette with anchovies & purple sprouting broccoli

Prep:10 mins **Cook:**15 mins

Serves 2

Ingredients

- 200g orecchiette
- 4 tbsp olive oil
- 6 anchovy fillets in oil, chopped (reserve 1 tbsp oil)
- 4 fat garlic cloves , thinly sliced
- 1 red chilli , thinly sliced
- zest 1 lemon , plus juice ½
- 50g fresh breadcrumb
- 200g purple sprouting broccoli

Method

STEP 1

Cook the orecchiette following pack instructions. Meanwhile, heat 3 tbsp of the olive oil and 1 tbsp of the oil from the anchovies in a frying pan. Add the garlic and chilli, and sizzle for 3-4 mins until the garlic is just starting to turn golden. Add the anchovies and lemon juice, and cook for 1-2 mins more until the anchovies melt into the sauce. Put the remaining olive oil, breadcrumbs and lemon zest in another frying pan, stir together and cook until crisp.

STEP 2

When the pasta has 4-5 mins to go, add the broccoli to the pan. When cooked, drain, reserving a cup of the pasta water, then add to the frying pan with the garlic and anchovies. Stir and cook over a low heat for a further 2 mins, adding a splash of pasta water if it looks dry. Season, then serve in pasta bowls with the lemony crumbs sprinkled over the top.

Low-fat chicken biryani

Prep:25 mins **Cook:**1 hr and 35 mins Plus marinating

Serves 5

Ingredients

- 3 garlic cloves , finely grated
- 2 tsp finely grated ginger
- ¼ tsp ground cinnamon
- 1 tsp turmeric
- 5 tbsp natural yogurt
- 600g boneless, skinless chicken breast , cut into 4-5cm pieces
- 2 tbsp semi-skimmed milk
- good pinch saffron
- 4 medium onions
- 4 tbsp rapeseed oil
- ½ tsp hot chilli powder
- 1 cinnamon stick , broken in half
- 5 green cardamom pods , lightly bashed to split

- 3 cloves
- 1 tsp cumin seed
- 280g basmati rice
- 700ml chicken stock
- 1 tsp garam masala
- handful chopped coriander leaves

Method

STEP 1

In a mixing bowl, stir together the garlic, ginger, cinnamon, turmeric and yogurt with some pepper and ¼ tsp salt. Tip in the chicken pieces and stir to coat (see step 1, above). Cover and marinate in the fridge for about 1 hr or longer if you have time. Warm the milk to tepid, stir in the saffron and set aside.

STEP 2

Heat oven to 200C/180C fan/gas 6. Slice each onion in half lengthways, reserve half and cut the other half into thin slices. Pour 1½ tbsp of the oil onto a baking tray, scatter over the sliced onion, toss to coat, then spread out in a thin, even layer (step 2). Roast for 40-45 mins, stirring halfway, until golden.

STEP 3

When the chicken has marinated, thinly slice the reserved onion. Heat 1 tbsp oil in a large sauté or frying pan. Fry the onion for 4-5 mins until golden. Stir in the chicken, a spoonful at a time, frying until it is no longer opaque, before adding the next spoonful (this helps to prevent the yogurt from curdling). Once the last of the chicken has been added, stir-fry for a further 5 mins until everything looks juicy. Scrape any sticky bits off the bottom of the pan, stir in the chilli powder, then pour in 100ml water, cover and simmer on a low heat for 15 mins. Remove and set aside.

STEP 4

Cook the rice while the chicken simmers. Heat another 1 tbsp oil in a large sauté pan, then drop in the cinnamon stick, cardamom, cloves and cumin seeds. Fry briefly until their aroma is released. Tip in the rice (step 3) and fry for 1 min, stirring constantly. Stir in the stock and bring to the boil. Lower the heat and simmer, covered, for about 8 mins or until all the stock has been absorbed. Remove from the heat and leave with the lid on for a few mins, so the rice can fluff up. Stir the garam masala into the remaining 1½ tsp oil and set aside. When the onions are roasted, remove and reduce oven to 180C/160C fan/gas 4.

STEP 5

Spoon half the chicken and its juices into an ovenproof dish, about 25 x 18 x 6cm, then scatter over a third of the roasted onions. Remove the whole spices from the rice, then layer half of the rice over the chicken and onions. Drizzle over the spiced oil. Spoon over the rest of the chicken and a third more onions. Top with the remaining rice (step 4) and drizzle over the saffron-infused milk. Scatter over the rest of the onions, cover tightly with foil and heat through in the oven for about 25 mins. Serve scattered with the mint and coriander.

Spicy meatballs with chilli black beans

Prep:20 mins **Cook:**25 mins

Serves 4

Ingredients

- 1 red onion, halved and sliced
- 2 garlic cloves, sliced
- 1 large yellow pepper, quartered, deseeded and diced
- 1 tsp ground cumin
- 2-3 tsp chipotle chilli paste
- 300ml reduced-salt chicken stock
- 400g can cherry tomatoes
- 400g can black beans or red kidney beans, drained
- 1 avocado, stoned, peeled and chopped
- juice ½ lime

For the meatballs

- 500g pack turkey breast mince
- 50g porridge oats
- 2 spring onions, finely chopped
- 1 tsp ground cumin
- 1 tsp coriander
- small bunch coriander, chopped, stalks and leaves kept separate

- 1 tsp rapeseed oil

Method

STEP 1

First make the meatballs. Tip the mince into a bowl, add the oats, spring onions, spices and the coriander stalks, then lightly knead the ingredients together until well mixed. Shape into 12 ping-pong- sized balls. Heat the oil in a non-stick frying pan, add the meatballs and cook, turning them frequently, until golden. Remove from the pan.

STEP 2

Tip the onion and garlic into the pan with the pepper and stir-fry until softened. Stir in the cumin and chilli paste, then pour in the stock. Return the meatballs to the pan and cook, covered, over a low heat for 10 mins. Stir in the tomatoes and beans, and cook, uncovered, for a few mins more. Toss the avocado chunks in the lime juice and serve the meatballs topped with the avocado and coriander leaves.

Slow cooker shepherd's pie

Prep:1 hr **Cook:**5 hrs

Serves 4

Ingredients

- 1 tbsp olive oil
- 1 onion, finely chopped
- 3-4 thyme sprigs
- 2 carrots, finely diced
- 250g lean (10%) mince lamb or beef
- 1 tbsp plain flour
- 1 tbsp tomato purée
- 400g can lentils, or white beans
- 1 tsp Worcestershire sauce

For the topping

- 650g potatoes, peeled and cut into chunks
- 250g sweet potatoes, peeled and cut into chunks

- 2 tbsp half-fat crème fraîche

Method

STEP 1

Heat the slow cooker if necessary. Heat the oil in a large frying pan. Tip the onions and thyme sprigs and fry for 2-3 mins. Then add the carrots and fry together, stirring occasionally until the vegetables start to brown. Stir in the mince and fry for 1-2 mins until no longer pink. Stir in the flour then cook for another 1-2 mins. Stir in the tomato purée and lentils and season with pepper and the Worcestershire sauce, adding a splash of water if you think the mixture is too dry. Scrape everything into the slow cooker.

STEP 2

Meanwhile cook both lots of potatoes in simmering water for 12-13 minutes or until they are cooked through. Drain well and then mash with the crème fraîche. Spoon this on top of the mince mixture and cook on Low for 5 hours - the mixture should be bubbling at the sides when it is ready. Crisp up the potato topping under the grill if you like.

Curried spinach, eggs & chickpeas

Prep:15 mins **Cook:**35 mins

Serves 2

Ingredients

- 1 tbsp rapeseed oil
- 1 onion , thinly sliced
- 1 garlic clove , crushed
- 3cm piece ginger , peeled and grated
- 1 tsp ground turmeric
- 1 tsp ground coriander
- 1 tsp garam masala
- 1 tbsp ground cumin
- 450g tomatoes , chopped
- 400g can chickpeas , drained
- 1 tsp sugar
- 200g spinach

- 2 large eggs
- 3 tbsp natural yogurt
- 1 red chilli , finely sliced
- ½ small bunch of coriander , torn

Method

STEP 1

Heat the oil in a large frying pan or flameproof casserole pot over a medium heat, and fry the onion for 10 mins until golden and sticky. Add the garlic, ginger, turmeric, ground coriander, garam masala, cumin and tomatoes, and fry for 2 mins more. Add the chickpeas, 100ml water and the sugar and bring to a simmer. Stir in the spinach, then cover and cook for 20-25 mins. Season to taste.

STEP 2

Cook the eggs in a pan of boiling water for 7 mins, then rinse under cold running water to cool. Drain, peel and halve. Swirl the yogurt into the curry, then top with the eggs, chilli and coriander. Season.

Cabbage soup

Prep:20 mins **Cook:**50 mins

Serves 6

Ingredients

- 2 tbsp olive oil
- 1 large onion , finely chopped
- 2 celery sticks , finely chopped
- 1 large carrot , finely chopped
- 70g smoked pancetta , diced (optional)
- 1 large Savoy cabbage , shredded
- 2 fat garlic cloves , crushed
- 1 heaped tsp sweet smoked paprika
- 1 tbsp finely chopped rosemary
- 1 x 400g can chopped tomatoes
- 1.7l hot vegetable stock

- 1 x 400g can chickpeas , drained and rinsed
- shaved parmesan (or vegetarian alternative), to serve (optional)
- crusty bread , to serve (optional)

Method

STEP 1

Heat the oil in a casserole pot over a low heat. Add the onion, celery and carrot, along with a generous pinch of salt, and fry gently for 15 mins, or until the veg begins to soften. If you're using pancetta, add it to the pan, turn up the heat and fry for a few mins more until turning golden brown. Tip in the cabbage and fry for 5 mins, then stir through the garlic, paprika and rosemary and cook for 1 min more.

STEP 2

Tip the chopped tomatoes and stock into the pan. Bring to a simmer, then cook, uncovered, for 30 mins, adding the chickpeas for the final 10 mins. Season generously with salt and black pepper.

STEP 3

Ladle the soup into six deep bowls. Serve with the shaved parmesan and crusty bread, if you like.

Red pepper, squash & harissa soup

Prep:15 mins **Cook:**1 hr

Serves 6

Ingredients

- 1 small butternut squash (about 600-700g), peeled and cut into chunks
- 2 red pepper , roughly chopped
- 2 red onion , roughly chopped
- 3 tbsp rapeseed oil
- 3 garlic cloves in their skins
- 1 tbsp ground coriander
- 2 tsp ground cumin
- 1.2l chicken or vegetable stock

- 2 tbsp harissa paste
- 50ml double cream

Method

STEP 1

Heat oven to 180C/160C fan/gas 4. Put all the veg on a large baking tray and toss together with rapeseed oil, garlic cloves in their skins, ground coriander, ground cumin and some seasoning. Roast for 45 mins, moving the veg around in the tray after 30 mins, until soft and starting to caramelise. Squeeze the garlic cloves out of their skins. Tip everything into a large pan. Add the chicken or vegetable stock, harissa paste and double cream. Bring to a simmer and bubble for a few mins. Blitz the soup in a blender, check the seasoning and add more liquid if you need to. Serve swirled with extra cream and harissa.

Warm cherry & brown sugar compote

Prep:5 mins **Cook:**15 mins

Serves 4

Ingredients

- 390g jar cherries in kirsch
- 2 tbsp dark brown sugar
- 4 big scoops of vanilla ice cream
- 50g amaretti biscuits

Method

STEP 1

Tip the cherries and sugar into a small saucepan. Bring to a simmer over a medium heat, stirring, and allow to bubble for 10 mins. Leave to cool slightly.

STEP 2

Scoop the ice cream into four bowls and pour over the warm compote. Crumble over the amaretti and serve.

Harissa-crumbed fish with lentils & peppers

Prep:15 mins **Cook:**15 mins

Serves 4

Ingredients

- 2 x 200g pouches cooked puy lentils
- 200g jar roasted red peppers , drained and torn into chunks
- 50g black olives , from a jar, roughly chopped
- 1 lemon , zested and cut into wedges
- 3 tbsp olive or rapeseed oil
- 4 x 140g cod fillets (or another white fish)
- 100g fresh breadcrumbs
- 1 tbsp harissa
- ½ small pack flat-leaf parsley , chopped

Method

STEP 1

Heat oven to 200C/180C fan/gas 6. Mix the lentils, peppers, olives, lemon zest, 2 tbsp oil and some seasoning in a roasting tin. Top with the fish fillets. Mix the breadcrumbs, harissa and the remaining oil and put a few spoonfuls on top of each piece of fish. Bake for 12-15 mins until the fish is cooked, the topping is crispy and the lentils are hot. Scatter with the parsley and squeeze over the lemon wedges.

Crispy Asian salmon with stir-fried noodles, pak choi & sugar snap peas

Prep:10 mins **Cook:**15 mins

Serves 2

Ingredients

- 2 x 100g salmon fillets (plus 2 more 100g salmon fillets if cooking for Flaked salmon salad lunch - see 'goes well with')
- For the marinade

- 2 tsp reduced salt tamari or soy sauce
- 2cm piece ginger, peeled and finely chopped or grated
- 1 garlic clove, finely chopped
- 2 tbsp lemon or lime juice
- 1 tsp sesame oil
- For the stir-fried noodles
- 85g vermicelli rice noodle
- 2 tsp rapeseed oil
- 1 tsp sesame oil
- 1 spring onion, trimmed and thinly sliced
- 1 garlic clove, finely chopped
- ½ red chilli, deseeded and finely chopped
- 2cm piece ginger, peeled and finely chopped
- 100g sugar snap pea
- 100g pak choi (or spinach)
- 1 large red pepper, sliced
- 1 tsp tamari or soy sauce
- 1 tsp Thai fish sauce
- juice ½ lime
- 1 tbsp finely chopped coriander

Method

STEP 1

Make the marinade by mixing together all the ingredients. Place the salmon fillets in a small bowl and spoon over the marinade, turning the fish so that it's nicely coated. Cover with cling film and leave to sit for 10 mins (or longer if you have time).

STEP 2

Meanwhile, cook the noodles following pack instructions, then drain and sit them in a bowl of cold water.

STEP 3

Heat a non-stick frying pan. Add the salmon fillets, skin-side down, and leave for 3 mins. When the fish is slightly crispy, flip over and cook for a further 3 mins on the other side. Just before you remove the fish from the pan, add any remaining marinade and let it sizzle for 10 secs.

Place 2 of the fillets, skin-side up, with their juices on a plate and cover with foil to keep warm. Put the other 2 fillets on another plate if using for Flaked salmon salad (see 'goes well with'), cover with foil, leave to cool, then chill.

STEP 4

In a frying pan or wok, heat the rapeseed and sesame oils over a high heat. Add the spring onion, garlic, chilli and ginger, and stir constantly for about 1 min. Add the sugar snap peas, pak choi and pepper, and stir for another 1-2 mins, then add the cooked noodles. Toss well, then add the soy sauce, fish sauce and lime juice, and mix until well combined and the pan is sizzling.

STEP 5

Remove from the heat and divide between 2 bowls. Top each with a salmon fillet and drizzle over any juices. Sprinkle with coriander and serve.

Turkey meatloaf

Prep:15 mins **Cook:**55 mins

Serves 4

Ingredients

- 1 tbsp olive oil
- 1 large onion , finely chopped
- 1 garlic clove , crushed
- 2 tbsp Worcestershire sauce
- 2 tsp tomato purée , plus 1 tbsp for the beans
- 500g turkey mince (thigh is best)
- 1 large egg , beaten
- 85g fresh white breadcrumbs
- 2 tbsp barbecue sauce , plus 4 tbsp for the beans
- 2 x 400g cans cannellini beans
- 1-2 tbsp roughly chopped parsley

Method

STEP 1

Heat oven to 180C/160C fan/gas 4. Heat the oil in a large frying pan and cook the onion for 8-10 mins until softened. Add the garlic, Worcestershire sauce and 2 tsp tomato purée, and stir until combined. Set aside to cool.

STEP 2

Put the turkey mince, egg, breadcrumbs and cooled onion mix in a large bowl and season well. Mix everything to combine, then shape into a rectangular loaf and place in a large roasting tin. Spread 2 tbsp barbecue sauce over the meatloaf and bake for 30 mins.

STEP 3

Meanwhile, drain 1 can of beans only, then pour both cans into a large bowl. Add the remaining barbecue sauce and tomato purée. Season and set aside.

STEP 4

When the meatloaf has had its initial cooking time, scatter the beans around the outside and bake for 15 mins more until the meatloaf is cooked through and the beans are piping hot. Scatter over the parsley and serve the meatloaf in slices.

Ginger, sesame and chilli prawn & broccoli stir-fry

Prep:5 mins **Cook:**10 mins

Serves 2

Ingredients

- 250g broccoli , thin-stemmed if you like, cut into even-sized florets
- 2 balls stem ginger , finely chopped, plus 2 tbsp syrup from the jar
- 3 tbsp low-salt soy sauce
- 1 garlic clove , crushed
- 1 red chilli , a little thinly sliced, the rest deseeded and finely chopped
- 2 tsp sesame seeds
- ½ tbsp sesame oil
- 200g raw king prawns
- 100g beansprouts
- cooked rice or noodles, to serve

Method

STEP 1

Heat a pan of water until boiling. Tip in the broccoli and cook for just 1 min – it should still have a good crunch. Meanwhile, mix the stem ginger and syrup, soy sauce, garlic and finely chopped chilli.

STEP 2

Toast the sesame seeds in a dry wok or large frying pan. When they're nicely browned, turn up the heat and add the oil, prawns and cooked broccoli. Stir-fry for a few mins until the prawns turn pink. Pour over the ginger sauce, then tip in the beansprouts. Cook for 30 seconds, or until the beansprouts are heated thoroughly, adding a splash more soy or ginger syrup, if you like. Scatter with the sliced chilli and serve over rice or noodles.

Paneer jalfrezi with cumin rice

Prep:20 mins **Cook:**30 mins

Serves 4

Ingredients

- 2 tsp cold-pressed rapeseed oil
- 1 large and 1 medium onion , large one finely chopped and medium one cut into wedges
- 2 large garlic cloves , chopped
- 50g ginger , peeled and shredded
- 2 tsp ground coriander
- 2 tsp cumin seeds
- 400g can chopped tomatoes
- 1 tbsp vegetable bouillon powder
- 135g paneer , chopped
- 2 large peppers , seeded and chopped
- 1 red or green chilli , deseeded and sliced
- 25g coriander , chopped

For the rice

- 260g brown basmati rice
- 1 tsp cumin seeds

Method

STEP 1

Heat 1 tsp oil a large non-stick frying pan and fry the chopped onions, garlic and half the ginger for 5 mins until softened. Add the ground coriander and cumin seeds and cook for 1 min more, then tip in the tomatoes, half a can of water and the bouillon. Blitz everything together with a stick blender until very smooth, then bring to a simmer. Cover and cook for 15 mins.

STEP 2

Meanwhile, cook the rice and cumin seeds in a pan of boiling water for 25 mins, or until tender.

STEP 3

Heat the remaining oil in a non-stick wok and fry the paneer until lightly coloured. Remove from the pan and set aside. Add the peppers, onion wedges and chilli to the pan and stir-fry until the veg is tender, but still retains some bite. Mix the stir-fried veg and paneer into the sauce with the chopped coriander, then serve with the rice. If you're following our Healthy Diet Plan, eat two portions of the curry and rice, then chill the rest for another day. Will keep for up to three days, covered, in the fridge. To serve on the second night, reheat the leftover portions in the microwave until piping hot.

Low 'n' slow rib steak with Cuban mojo salsa

Prep:20 mins **Cook:**3 hrs and 20 mins

Serves 2

Ingredients

- 1 rib steak on the bone or côte du boeuf (about 800g)
- 1 tbsp rapeseed oil
- 1 garlic clove
- 2 thyme sprigs
- 25g butter , chopped into small pieces
- sweet potato fries
- a dressed salad , to serve

For the mojo salsa

- 2 limes
- 1 small orange
- ½ small bunch mint , finely chopped
- small bunch coriander , finely chopped
- 4 spring onions , finely chopped
- 1 small garlic clove , crushed
- 1 fat green chilli , finely chopped
- 4 tbsp extra virgin rapeseed oil or olive oil

Method

STEP 1

Leave the beef at room temperature for about 1 hr before you cook it. Heat oven to 60C/40C fan/gas 1 /4 if you like your beef medium rare, or 65C/45C fan/gas 1 /4 for medium. (Cooking at these low temperatures will be more accurate in an electric oven than in a gas one. If using gas, put the oven on the lowest setting you have, and be aware that the cooking time may be shorter.)

STEP 2

Put the unseasoned beef in a heavy-based ovenproof frying pan. Cook in the middle of the oven for 3 hrs undisturbed.

STEP 3

Meanwhile, make the salsa. Zest the limes and orange into a bowl. Cut each in half and place, cut-side down, in a hot pan. Cook for a few mins until the fruits are charred, then squeeze the juice into the bowl. Add the other ingredients and season well.

STEP 4

When the beef is cooked, it should look dry on the surface, and dark pink in colour. If you have a meat thermometer, test the internal temperature – it should be 58-60C. Remove the pan from the oven and set over a high heat on the hob. Add the oil and sear the meat on both sides for a few mins until caramelised. Sear the fat for a few mins too. Smash the garlic clove with the heel of your hand and add this to the pan with the thyme and butter. When the butter is foaming, spoon it over the beef and cook for another 1-2 mins. Transfer the beef to a warm plate, cover with foil, and leave to rest for 5-10 mins. Carve away from the bone and into slices before serving with the salsa, fries and salad.

Asparagus & broad bean lasagne

Prep:35 mins **Cook:**1 hr and 10 mins

Serves 4

Ingredients

- 225ml whole milk
- 320g frozen baby broad beans
- 3 garlic cloves , chopped
- 30g pack fresh basil , roughly chopped
- ½ lemon , zested
- 4 spring onions , chopped
- 1 tsp vegetable bouillon powder
- 6 wholemeal lasagne sheets
- 320g frozen peas
- 2 x 300g tubs low-fat cottage cheese
- 1 egg
- whole nutmeg , for grating
- 250g asparagus , woody ends trimmed
- 25g parmesan or vegetarian alternative, finely grated

Method

STEP 1

Heat oven to 180C/160C fan/gas 4. Heat the milk in a pan until just boiling, then tip in the beans (add a splash of water to cover if you need to). Cook for 3 mins to defrost, then add the garlic, basil, lemon zest, spring onions and bouillon, then blitz for a few mins with a hand blender until smooth.

STEP 2

Spoon half the purée into a 20 x 26cm ovenproof dish. Top with 3 lasagne sheets, the remaining purée, and the peas, then the remaining lasagne sheets.

STEP 3

Whisk the cottage cheese with the egg and a good grating of nutmeg. Pour over the lasagne, then press in the asparagus and scatter over the parmesan. Bake for 1 hr until golden and a knife easily slides through. Can be kept chilled for two days.

Smoky chickpeas on toast

Prep:2 mins **Cook:**10 mins

Serves 2

Ingredients

- 1 tsp olive oil or vegetable oil, plus a drizzle
- 1 small onion or banana shallot, chopped
- 2 tsp chipotle paste
- 250ml passata
- 400g can chickpeas , drained
- 2 tsp honey
- 2 tsp red wine vinegar
- 2-4 slices good crusty bread
- 2 eggs

Method

STEP 1

Heat ½ tsp of the oil in a pan. Tip in the onion and cook until soft, about 5-8 mins, then add the chipotle paste, passata, chickpeas, honey and vinegar. Season and bubble for 5 mins.

STEP 2

Toast the bread. Heat the remaining oil in a frying pan and fry the eggs. Drizzle the toast with a little oil, then top with the chickpeas and fried eggs.

Charred aubergine salad with sugar-spice onions

Prep:30 mins **Cook:**1 hr

Serves 4 as a main course, 8 as a side

Ingredients

- 1 large aubergine , thinly sliced into rounds
- 1-2 tbsp sunflower oil
- 50g desiccated coconut
- ½ tsp turmeric
- 2 x 400g cans brown lentils , rinsed and drained
- bunch spring onions , sliced
- small pack coriander , stalks finely chopped, leaves roughly chopped
- 150g pack pomegranate seeds
- 85g cashew nuts , bashed a few times

For the sugar-spice onions

- 3 onions , roughly sliced
- 1 tbsp sunflower oil
- 2 tsp each ground cumin
- 2 tsp ground coriander
- 2 tbsp light brown soft sugar

For the dressing

- 160ml can coconut cream
- juice 3 limes
- ½ tsp turmeric
- 1 tbsp onion seeds or nigella seeds
- 2 tbsp mango chutney

Method

STEP 1

Start with the sugar-spice onions. Put the onions, oil, 1/2 tsp salt and the spices in a frying pan and cook gently for 15 mins until really soft. Stir in the sugar and cook for a futher 2-3 mins until the onions are sticky and dark golden.

STEP 2

Meanwhile, heat a griddle pan over a medium heat and brush the aubergine slices on both sides with the oil. Griddle in batches, turning, until charred and soft.

STEP 3

Once the onions are cooked, tip them onto a plate and leave to cool. Clean the pan, tip in the coconut and turmeric, and toast gently until golden and just browning at the edges. Tip onto a plate and leave to cool. Whisk together all the dressing ingredients with some seasoning.

STEP 4

To serve, tip the lentils, spring onions, coriander, pomegranate seeds and cashew nuts onto a big serving platter or bowl. Add most of the coconut, plus the aubergine slices and sugar-spice onions. Drizzle over most of the dressing and use your hands to toss everything together well. Scatter the remaining coconut over to serve, with the extra dressing on the side for drizzling over.

Sugared scones

Prep:20 mins **Cook:**12 mins

Makes about 8

Ingredients

- 85g diced butter
- 350g self-raising flour
- ¼ tsp salt
- 1 ½ tsp bicarbonate of soda
- 4 tbsp caster sugar
- 200ml milk , warmed to room temperature, plus a splash extra
- crushed sugar cubes , to decorate

Method

STEP 1

Heat oven to 200C/180C fan/gas 6. Whizz butter into flour. Tip into a bowl and stir in salt with bicarbonate of soda and sugar. Using a cutlery knife, quickly stir in milk – don't over-mix.

STEP 2

Tip out onto a lightly floured surface and turn over a couple of times to very gently bring together with your hands. Gently pat to about 1in thick, then stamp out rounds with a floured cutter. Pat together trimmings to stamp out more. Brush the tops with a splash more milk, then scatter with crushed sugar cubes. Bake on a baking sheet for 10-12 mins until risen and golden.

Healthy bolognese

Prep:5 mins **Cook:**20 mins

2 generously, 4 as a snack

Ingredients

- 100g wholewheat linguine
- 2 tsp rapeseed oil
- 1 fennel bulb , finely chopped
- 2 garlic cloves , sliced
- 200g pork mince with less than 5% fat
- 200g whole cherry tomatoes
- 1 tbsp balsamic vinegar
- 1 tsp vegetable bouillon powder
- generous handful chopped basil

Method

STEP 1

Bring a large pan of water to the boil, then cook the linguine following pack instructions, about 10 mins.

STEP 2

Meanwhile, heat the oil in a non-stick wok or wide pan. Add the fennel and garlic and cook, stirring every now and then, until tender, about 10 mins.

STEP 3

Tip in the pork and stir-fry until it changes colour, breaking it up as you go so there are no large clumps. Add the tomatoes, vinegar and bouillon, then cover the pan and cook for 10 mins over a low heat until the tomatoes burst and the pork is cooked and tender. Add the linguine and basil and plenty of pepper, and toss well before serving.

Fennel spaghetti

Prep:15 mins **Cook:**30 mins

Serves 2

Ingredients

- 1 tbsp olive oil , plus extra for serving
- 1 tsp fennel seeds
- 2 small garlic cloves , 1 crushed, 1 thinly sliced
- 1 lemon , zested and juiced
- 1 fennel bulb , finely sliced, fronds reserved
- 150g spaghetti
- ½ pack flat-leaf parsley , chopped
- shaved parmesan (or vegetarian alternative), to serve (optional)

Method

STEP 1

Heat the oil in a frying pan over a medium heat and cook the fennel seeds until they pop. Sizzle the garlic for 1 min, then add the lemon zest and half the fennel slices. Cook for 10-12 mins or until the fennel has softened.

STEP 2

Meanwhile, bring a pan of salted water to the boil and cook the pasta for 1 min less than pack instructions. Use tongs to transfer the pasta to the frying pan along with a good splash of pasta water. Increase the heat to high and toss well. Stir through the remaining fennel slices, the parsley and lemon juice, season generously, then tip straight into two bowls to serve. Top with the fennel fronds, extra olive oil and parmesan shavings, if you like.

Vietnamese chicken noodle soup

Prep:20 mins **Cook:**25 mins

Serves 6

Ingredients

- 1 tbsp vegetable oil
- 3 shallots, sliced

- 3 garlic cloves, sliced
- 1 lemongrass stalk, chopped
- 2.5cm piece ginger, sliced
- 3 star anise
- 1 cinnamon stick
- 1 tsp coriander seeds
- ¼ tsp Chinese five spice
- ¼ tsp black peppercorns
- 1 tsp caster sugar
- 1 tbsp fish sauce
- 1.25 - 1.5 litres good quality fresh chicken stock
- 3 large chicken breasts (about 500g)

To serve

- 450g rice noodles
- 4 spring onions, finely sliced on an angle
- 1 carrot, shredded or peeled into ribbon with a vegetable peeler
- 2 large handfuls (150g) mung bean sprouts
- large bunch coriander, chopped
- small bunch mint, leaves chopped
- 1 red chilli, thinly sliced (optional)
- 2 tbsp crispy fried shallots (optional)
- 1 kaffir lime leaf, tough central stalk removed, very finely sliced, (optional)
- 1 lime, cut into wedges

Method

STEP 1

Heat the oil in a small frying pan on medium heat and gently cook the shallots and garlic until caramelised and golden brown (about 4-5 mins).

STEP 2

In a large saucepan, add the caramelised shallots and garlic, lemongrass, ginger, star anise, cinnamon stick, coriander seeds, Chinese five-spice, peppercorns, sugar, fish sauce, chicken stock and chicken breasts. Cover with a lid and bring to a very gentle simmer for about 15 mins.

STEP 3

Meanwhile, cook the noodles, following pack instructions, until just cooked through (do not over-cook). Rinse under cold water to prevent them sticking together. Drain and divide between serving bowls.

STEP 4

Strain the soup through a sieve. Discard the spices. Shred the chicken and keep to one side. Return soup to the pot and bring to a boil. Season to taste with more fish sauce if needed.

STEP 5

To serve, ladle piping hot soup into bowls of noodles and chicken, and top with spring onion, carrot, bean sprouts, and herbs, plus the chilli, crispy shallots and kaffir lime leaf if using. Serve with a lime wedge to squeeze over, and more fish sauce and chilli to taste.

Broccoli pasta shells

Prep:5 mins **Cook:**15 mins

Serves 4

Ingredients

- 1 head of broccoli, chopped into florets
- 1 garlic clove, unpeeled
- 2 tbsp olive oil
- 250g pasta shells
- ½ small pack parsley
- ½ small pack basil
- 30g toasted pine nuts
- ½ lemon, zested and juiced
- 30g parmesan (or vegetarian alternative), plus extra to serve

Method

STEP 1

Heat the oven to 200C/180C fan/gas 6. Toss the broccoli and garlic in 1 tbsp of the olive oil on a roasting tray and roast in the oven for 10-12 mins, until softened.

STEP 2

Tip the pasta shells into a pan of boiling, salted water. Cook according to packet instructions and drain. Tip the parsley, basil, pine nuts, lemon juice and parmesan into a blender. Once the broccoli is done, set aside a few of the smaller pieces. Squeeze the garlic from its skin, add to the blender along with the rest of the broccoli, pulse to a pesto and season well.

STEP 3

Toss the pasta with the pesto. Add the reserved broccoli florets, split between two bowls and top with a little extra parmesan, the lemon zest and a good grinding of black pepper, if you like.

Chilli chicken wraps

Prep:10 mins **Cook:**25 mins

Serves 4

Ingredients

- 2 tbsp vegetable oil
- 6 boneless, skinless chicken thighs, cut into bite-sized pieces
- 1 large onion, thinly sliced into half-moons
- 2 garlic cloves, finely chopped
- 3cm piece ginger, peeled and finely chopped
- ½ tsp ground cumin
- ½ tsp garam masala
- 1 tbsp tomato purée
- 1 red chilli, thinly sliced into rings
- juice ½ lemon
- 4 rotis, warmed
- ½ small red onion, chopped
- 4 tbsp mango chutney or lime pickle
- 4 handfuls mint or coriander
- 4 tbsp yogurt

Method

STEP 1

Heat the oil in a large frying pan over a medium heat. Add the chicken, brown on all sides, then remove. Add the onion, garlic, ginger and a pinch of salt. Cook for 5 mins or until softened.

STEP 2

Increase the heat to high. Return the chicken to the pan with the spices, tomato purée, chilli and lemon juice. Season well and cook for 10 mins or until the chicken is tender.

STEP 3

Divide the chicken, red onion, chutney, herbs and yogurt between the four warm rotis. Roll up and serve with plenty of napkins

Squash & spinach fusilli with pecans

Prep:10 mins **Cook:**40 mins

Serves 2

Ingredients

- 160g butternut squash , diced
- 3 garlic cloves , sliced
- 1 tbsp chopped sage leaves
- 2 tsp rapeseed oil
- 1 large courgette , halved and sliced
- 6 pecan halves
- 115g wholemeal fusilli
- 125g bag baby spinach

Method

STEP 1

Heat oven to 200C/180C fan/gas 6. Toss the butternut squash, garlic and sage in the oil, then spread out in a roasting tin and cook in the oven for 20 mins, add the courgettes and cook for a further 15 mins. Give everything a stir, then add the pecans and cook for 5 mins more until the nuts are toasted and the vegetables are tender and starting to caramelise.

STEP 2

Meanwhile, boil the pasta according to pack instructions – about 12 mins. Drain, then tip into a serving bowl and toss with the spinach so that it wilts in the heat from the pasta. Add the roasted veg and pecans, breaking up the nuts a little, and toss again really well before serving.

Sali murghi

Prep:20 mins **Cook:**55 mins

Serves 6 - 8

Ingredients

- 2½ tbsp ghee or vegetable oil
- 8 chicken thighs
- 1 cinnamon stick
- 5 green cardamom pods , bashed, seeds removed
- 1 tsp cumin seeds
- 2 onions , finely chopped
- 2 green chillies , roughly chopped
- 3 garlic cloves , roughly chopped
- 5cm piece ginger , roughly chopped
- 1 tsp ground coriander
- 1 tsp ground garam masala
- 1 tsp Kashmiri chilli powder
- ½ tsp turmeric
- 3 medium tomatoes , around 300g, finely chopped (or blitzed)
- 2 tbsp white wine vinegar
- 2 tsp jaggery (or soft brown sugar)
- 150g dried apricots (use the soft, ready-to-eat type)
- ½ small pack coriander , chopped
- Sali (optional)
- 1 large potato , peeled and sliced into matchsticks (see tip below)
- vegetable oil , for shallow frying

Method

STEP 1

Melt 1 tbsp of the ghee in a pan and add the chicken, skin-side side down. Once the skin is golden and crisp (around 5 mins), remove from the pan and set aside (you may need to do this in batches). Melt the remaining ghee in the pan, add the cinnamon, cardamom and cumin seeds, and fry until fragrant – around 5 mins. Stir in the onions along with a big pinch of salt and fry for 5 mins until browning in places.

STEP 2

Blitz the green chilli with the garlic and ginger, add to the pan and cook for 2 more mins, then stir in the spices and cook for a few mins more, splashing in a little water to prevent the spices from sticking. Tip in the chopped tomatoes.

STEP 3

Return the chicken to the pan, coating it with the curry base, then splash in the white wine vinegar followed by the jaggery. Add 100ml water, then cover and simmer for 30 mins. Remove the lid and stir in the apricots and coriander, then cook for 10-15 mins longer, until the gravy reduces.

STEP 4

Meanwhile, make the sali. Pat the potato matchsticks dry with kitchen paper. Pour vegetable oil into a small, deep saucepan until it's a few cm deep, and heat over a medium-high heat. Add a handful of the potato matchsticks at a time and fry for around a minute, until golden and crisp. Remove with a slotted spoon, drain on kitchen paper and season generously. Serve the curry with the sali piled on top.

Asparagus & lemon spaghetti with peas

Prep:7 mins **Cook:**12 mins

Serves 2

Ingredients

- 150g wholemeal spaghetti
- 160g asparagus, ends trimmed and cut into lengths
- 2 tbsp rapeseed oil
- 2 leeks (220g), cut into lengths, then thin strips
- 1 red chilli, deseeded and finely chopped
- 1 garlic clove, finely grated

- 160g frozen peas
- 1 lemon, zested and juiced, plus wedges to serve

Method

STEP 1

Boil the spaghetti for 12 mins until al dente, adding the asparagus for the last 3 mins. Meanwhile, heat the oil in a large non-stick frying pan, add the leeks and chilli and cook for 5 mins. Stir in the garlic, peas and lemon zest and juice and cook for a few mins more.

STEP 2

Drain and add the pasta to the pan with ¼ mug of the pasta water and toss everything together until well mixed. Spoon into shallow bowls and serve with lemon wedges for squeezing over, if you like.

Courgette, leek & goat's cheese soup

Prep:8 mins **Cook:**17 mins

Serves 4

Ingredients

- 1 tbsp rapeseed oil
- 400g leeks, well washed and sliced
- 450g courgettes, sliced
- 3 tsp vegetable bouillon powder, made up to 1 litre with boiling water
- 400g spinach
- 150g tub soft vegetarian goat's cheese
- 15g basil, plus a few leaves to serve
- 8 tsp omega seed mix (see tip)
- 4 x 25g portions wholegrain rye bread

Method

STEP 1

Heat the oil in a large pan and fry the leeks for a few mins to soften. Add the courgettes, then cover the pan and cook for 5 mins more. Pour in the stock, cover and cook for about 7 mins.

STEP 2

Add the spinach, then cover the pan and cook for 5 mins so that it wilts. Take off the heat and blitz until really smooth with a hand blender. Add the goat's cheese and basil, then blitz again.

STEP 3

If you're making this recipe as part of our two-person Summer Healthy Diet Plan, spoon half the soup into two bowls or large flasks, then cool and chill the remainder for another day. Reheat in a pan or microwave to serve. If serving in bowls, scatter with some extra basil leaves and the seeds, and eat with the rye bread.

Low-fat moussaka

Prep:15 mins **Cook:**40 mins

Serves 4

Ingredients

- 200g frozen sliced peppers
- 3 garlic cloves , crushed
- 200g extra-lean minced beef
- 100g red lentils
- 2 tsp dried oregano , plus extra for sprinkling
- 500ml carton passata
- 1 aubergine , sliced into 1.5cm rounds
- 4 tomatoes , sliced into 1cm rounds
- 2 tsp olive oil
- 25g parmesan , finely grated
- 170g pot 0% fat Greek yogurt
- freshly grated nutmeg

Method

STEP 1

Cook the peppers gently in a large non-stick pan for about 5 mins – the water from them should stop them sticking. Add the garlic and cook for 1 min more, then add the beef, breaking up with a fork, and cook until brown. Tip in the lentils, half the oregano, the passata and a splash of water. Simmer for 15-20 mins until the lentils are tender, adding more water if you need to.

STEP 2

Meanwhile, heat the grill to Medium. Arrange the aubergine and tomato slices on a non-stick baking tray and brush with the oil. Sprinkle with the remaining oregano and some seasoning, then grill for 1-2 mins each side until lightly charred – you may need to do this in batches.

STEP 3

Mix half the Parmesan with the yogurt and some seasoning. Divide the beef mixture between 4 small ovenproof dishes and top with the sliced aubergine and tomato. Spoon over the yogurt topping and sprinkle with the extra oregano, Parmesan and nutmeg. Grill for 3-4 mins until bubbling. Serve with a salad, if you like.

Salmon salad with sesame dressing

Prep:7 mins **Cook:**16 mins

Serves 2

Ingredients

For the salad

- 250g new potatoes , sliced
- 160g French beans , trimmed
- 2 wild salmon fillets
- 80g salad leaves
- 4 small clementines , 3 sliced, 1 juiced
- handful of basil , chopped
- handful of coriander , chopped

For the dressing

- 2 tsp sesame oil
- 2 tsp tamari
- ½ lemon , juiced
- 1 red chilli , deseeded and chopped
- 2 tbsp finely chopped onion (1/4 small onion)

Method

STEP 1

Steam the potatoes and beans in a steamer basket set over a pan of boiling water for 8 mins. Arrange the salmon fillets on top and steam for a further 6-8 mins, or until the salmon flakes easily when tested with a fork.

STEP 2

Meanwhile, mix the dressing ingredients together along with the clementine juice. If eating straightaway, divide the salad leaves between two plates and top with the warm potatoes and beans and the clementine slices. Arrange the salmon fillets on top, scatter over the herbs and spoon over the dressing. If taking to work, prepare the potatoes, beans and salmon the night before, then pack into a rigid airtight container with the salad leaves kept separate. Put the salad elements together and dress just before eating to prevent the leaves from wilting.

Cod with cucumber, avocado & mango salsa salad

Prep:5 mins **Cook:**8 mins

Serves 2

Ingredients

- 2 x skinless cod fillets
- 1 lime , zested and juiced
- 1 small mango , peeled, stoned and chopped (or 2 peaches, stoned and chopped)
- 1 small avocado , stoned, peeled and sliced
- ¼ cucumber , chopped
- 160g cherry tomatoes , quartered

- 1 red chilli , deseeded and chopped
- 2 spring onions , sliced
- handful chopped coriander

Method

STEP 1

Heat oven to 200C/180C fan/gas 6. Put the fish in a shallow ovenproof dish and pour over half the lime juice, with a little of the zest, then grind over some black pepper. Bake for 8 mins or until the fish flakes easily but is still moist.

STEP 2

Meanwhile, put the rest of the ingredients, plus the remaining lime juice and zest, in a bowl and combine well. Spoon onto plates and top with the cod, spooning over any juices in the dish.

Easter biscuits

Prep:1 hr and 15 mins **Cook:**30 mins

makes 18

Ingredients

- 300g plain flour , plus extra for dusting
- 150g white caster sugar
- 150g slightly salted butter , chopped
- 1 large egg
- 2 tsp vanilla extract or vanilla bean paste

For the iced option

- 500g royal icing sugar
- your favourite food colouring gels
- For the jammy middle option
- icing sugar , for dusting
- 400g apricot jam , or lemon curd

Method

STEP 1

Weigh the flour and sugar in a bowl. Add the butter and rub together with your fingertips until the mixture resembles wet sand, with no buttery lumps. Beat the egg with the vanilla, then add to the bowl. Mix briefly with a cutlery knife to combine, then use your hands to knead the dough together – try not to overwork the dough, or the biscuits will be tough. Shape into a disc, then wrap in cling film and chill for at least 15 mins. Heat oven to 180C/160C fan/gas 4. Line two baking sheets with baking parchment.

STEP 2

Dust a work surface with flour. Halve the dough, then roll one half out to the thickness of a £1 coin. Use an egg-shaped cookie cutter (ours was 10cm long; you could also make a cardboard template to cut around) to stamp out as many cookies as you can, then transfer them to one of the baking sheets, leaving a little space between the biscuits. Repeat with the other half of the dough. If you want to make jammy biscuits, use a small circular cutter to stamp holes in half of the biscuits (where the yolk would be). If you intend to make both iced and jammy biscuits, only stamp holes in a quarter of the biscuits.

STEP 3

Bake for 12-15 mins, until the biscuits are pale gold. Cool on the sheets for 10 mins, then transfer to a wire rack to cool fully. Once cool, decorate to your liking (see next steps). Will keep in an airtight container for up to five days.

STEP 4

To decorate the biscuits with icing, add enough water to the icing sugar to make a thick icing – it should hold its shape without spreading when piped. Transfer about a third of the icing to a piping bag fitted with a very small round nozzle (or just snip a tiny opening at the tip). Pipe an outline around the biscuits, then draw patterns in the middle – lines, spots and zigzags work well. Leave to dry for 10 mins. Divide the remaining icing between as many colours as you'd like to use, then use the gels to dye them. Loosen each icing with a few drops of water, then transfer them to piping bags. Use the coloured icing to fill the empty spaces on the biscuits. You may need to use a cocktail stick to tease it into the corners. Once covered, leave to dry for a few hours.

STEP 5

To make the jammy middle biscuits, dust the biscuits with holes in the middle with a heavy coating of icing sugar. Spread the jam or curd generously over the whole biscuits, then sandwich the dusted biscuits on top of them.

Ginger chicken & green bean noodles

Prep:10 mins **Cook:**15 mins

Serves 2

Ingredients

- ½ tbsp vegetable oil
- 2 skinless chicken breasts, sliced
- 200g green beans , trimmed and halved crosswise
- thumb-sized piece of ginger , peeled and cut into matchsticks
- 2 garlic cloves , sliced
- 1 ball stem ginger , finely sliced, plus 1 tsp syrup from the jar
- 1 tsp cornflour , mixed with 1 tbsp water
- 1 tsp dark soy sauce , plus extra to serve (optional)
- 2 tsp rice vinegar
- 200g cooked egg noodles

Method

STEP 1

Heat the oil in a wok over a high heat and stir-fry the chicken for 5 mins. Add the green beans and stir-fry for 4-5 mins more until the green beans are just tender, and the chicken is just cooked through.

STEP 2

Stir in the fresh ginger and garlic, and stir-fry for 2 mins, then add the stem ginger and syrup, the cornflour mix, soy sauce and vinegar. Stir-fry for 1 min, then toss in the noodles. Cook until everything is hot and the sauce coats the noodles. Drizzle with more soy, if you like, and serve.

Potato, pea & egg curry rotis

Prep:5 mins **Cook:**25 mins

Serves 4

Ingredients

- 1 tbsp oil
- 2 tbsp mild curry paste
- 400g can chopped tomatoes
- 2 potatoes , cut into small chunks
- 200g peas
- 3 eggs , hard-boiled
- pack rotis , warmed through
- 150g tub natural yogurt , to serve

Method

STEP 1

Heat the oil in a saucepan and briefly fry the curry paste. Tip in the tomatoes and half a can of water and bring to a simmer. Add the potatoes and cook for 20 mins, or until the potato is tender. Stir in the peas and cook for 3 mins.

STEP 2

Halve the eggs and place them on top of the curry, then warm everything through. Serve with the rotis and yogurt on the side.

Sugar-crusted bara brith

Prep:15 mins **Cook:**1 hr - 1 hr and 15 mins Plus overnight soaking

Serves 12

Ingredients

- 400g/14oz luxury mixed fruit
- 75g pack dried cranberries
- mug hot strong black tea
- 100g butter , plus extra for greasing
- 2 heaped tbsp orange marmalade

- 2 eggs , beaten
- 450g self-raising flour - try a mix of wholemeal and white
- 175g light soft brown sugar
- 1 tsp each ground cinnamon and ground ginger
- 4 tbsp milk
- 50g crushed sugar cubes or granulated sugar, to decorate

Method

STEP 1

Mix together the dried fruit and cranberries in a large bowl, then pour the hot tea over. Cover with cling film and leave to soak overnight.

STEP 2

Heat oven to 180C/fan 160C/gas 4. Butter and line the bottom of a 900g/2lb loaf tin with baking parchment. Melt butter and marmalade together in a pan. Leave to cool for 5 mins, then beat in the eggs. Drain any excess tea from the fruit. Mix the flour, sugar and spices together, then stir in the fruit, butter mix and milk until evenly combined. The batter should softly drop from the spoon – add more milk if needed.

STEP 3

Spoon into the tin and level the top. Sprinkle with the crushed sugar and bake for 1-1¼ hrs until dark golden and a skewer inserted comes out clean. Cover loosely with foil if it starts to over-colour before the middle is cooked. Leave to cool completely in the tin and serve sliced.

Thai prawn & ginger noodles

Prep:15 mins **Cook:**15 mins plus soaking

Serves 2

Ingredients

- 100g folded rice noodles (sen lek)
- zest and juice 1 small orange
- 1½-2 tbsp red curry paste
- 1-2 tsp fish sauce
- 2 tsp light brown soft sugar

- 1 tbsp sunflower oil
- 25g ginger, scraped and shredded
- 2 large garlic cloves, sliced
- 1 red pepper, deseeded and sliced
- 85g sugar snap peas, halved lengthways
- 140g beansprouts
- 175g pack raw king prawns
- handful chopped basil
- handful chopped coriander

Method

STEP 1

Put the noodles in a bowl and pour over boiling water to cover them. Set aside to soak for 10 mins. Stir together the orange juice and zest, curry paste, fish sauce, sugar and 3 tbsp water to make a sauce.

STEP 2

Heat the oil in a large wok and add half the ginger and the garlic. Cook, stirring, for 1 min. Add the pepper and stir-fry for 3 mins more. Toss in the sugar snaps, cook briefly, then pour in the curry sauce. Add the beansprouts and prawns, and continue cooking until the prawns just turn pink. Drain the noodles, then toss these into the pan with the herbs and remaining ginger. Mix until the noodles are well coated in the sauce, then serve.

Easy soup maker lentil soup

Prep:5 mins **Cook:**30 mins

Serves 4

Ingredients

- 750ml vegetable or ham stock
- 75g red lentils
- 3 carrots , finely chopped
- 1 medium leek , sliced (150g)
- small handful chopped parsley , to serve

Method

STEP 1

Put the stock, lentils, carrots and leek into a soup maker, and press the 'chunky soup' function. Make sure you don't fill it above the max fill line. The soup will look a little foamy to start, but don't worry – it will disappear once cooked.

STEP 2

Once the cycle is complete, check the lentils are tender, and season well. Scatter over the parsley to serve.

Frosé

Prep:5 mins(plus freezing overnight) **Serves 4-6**

Ingredients

- 1 bottle dry rosé
- 300g strawberries , hulled and halved
- 50g caster sugar
- juice of 1 lemon

Method

STEP 1

Pour the bottle of rosé into a deep roasting tin and carefully put it in the freezer overnight.

STEP 2

The next day, mix the strawberries with the sugar and leave to sit for 30 mins until the strawberries begin to release their juices.

STEP 3

Blend the frozen rosé, strawberries, sugar and lemon juice together, then divide between glasses for the ultimate refreshing summer cocktail.

Asian tofu with stir-fried noodles, pak choi & sugar snap peas

Prep:10 mins **Cook:**15 mins plus marinatingq

Serves 2

Ingredients

- 195g extra-firm tofu

For the marinade

- 2 tsp tamari or soy sauce
- 2cm piece ginger , peeled and finely chopped or grated
- 1 garlic clove , finely chopped
- 2 tbsp lemon or lime juice
- 1 tsp sesame oil

For the stir-fried noodles

- 85g vermicelli rice noodle
- 2 tsp rapeseed oil
- 1 tsp sesame oil
- 1 spring onion , trimmed and thinly sliced
- 1 garlic clove , finely chopped
- ½ red chilli , deseeded and finely chopped
- 2cm piece ginger , peeled and finely chopped
- 100g sugar snap pea
- 100g pak choi (or spinach)
- 1 large red pepper , sliced
- 1 tsp tamari or soy sauce
- juice ½ lime
- 1 tbsp finely chopped coriander

Method

STEP 1

Make the marinade by mixing together all the ingredients. Drain the tofu by placing on several sheets of kitchen paper on a plate, with several more on top, and a heavy weight (such as a pan) on top of that. Leave for at least 15 mins. Cut the tofu into cubes and put in a small bowl with the marinade. Cover and leave for 30 mins-1 hr.

STEP 2

Meanwhile, cook the noodles following pack instructions, then drain and sit them in a bowl of cold water.

STEP 3

Heat a non-stick frying pan. Add the tofu pieces and fry until hot and crispy. Just before you remove the tofu from the pan, add any remaining marinade and let it sizzle for 10 secs. Place the tofu on a plate and cover with foil to keep warm.

STEP 4

In a frying pan or wok, heat the rapeseed and sesame oils over a high heat. Add the spring onion, garlic, chilli and ginger, and stir constantly for about 1 min. Add the sugar snap peas, pak choi and pepper, and stir for another 1-2 mins, then add the cooked noodles. Toss well, then add the soy sauce and lime juice, and mix until well combined and the pan is sizzling.

STEP 5

Remove from the heat and divide between 2 bowls. Top each with tofu cubes and drizzle over any juices. Sprinkle with coriander and serve.

Slow cooker mushroom risotto

Prep:30 mins **Cook:**1 hr

Serves 4

Ingredients

- 1 onion, finely chopped
- 1 tsp olive oil
- 250g chestnut mushrooms, sliced
- 1l vegetable stock

- 50g porcini
- 300g wholegrain rice
- small bunch parsley, finely chopped
- grated vegetarian parmesan-style cheese to serve

Method

STEP 1

Heat the slow cooker if necessary. Fry the onion in the oil in a frying pan with a splash of water for 10 minutes or until it is soft but not coloured. Add the mushroom slices and stir them around until they start to soften and release their juices.

STEP 2

Meanwhile pour the stock into a saucepan and add the porcini, bring to a simmer and then leave to soak. Tip the onions and mushrooms into the slow cooker and add the rice, stir it in well. Pour over the stock and porcini leaving any bits of sediment in the saucepan (or pour the mixture through a fine sieve).

STEP 3

Cook on High for 3 hours, stirring halfway. and then check the consistency – the rice should be cooked. If it needs a little more liquid stir in a splash of stock. Stir in the parsley and season. Serve with the parmesan.

Hake & seafood cataplana

Prep:15 mins **Cook:**35 mins

Serves 2

Ingredients

- 2 tbsp cold-pressed rapeseed oil
- 1 onion , halved and thinly sliced
- 250g salad potatoes , cut into chunks
- 1 large red pepper , deseeded and chopped
- 1 courgette (200g), thickly sliced
- 2 tomatoes , chopped (150g)
- 2 large garlic cloves , finely grated

- 1 tbsp cider vinegar (optional)
- 2 tsp vegetable bouillon powder
- 2 skinless hake fillets (pack size 240g)
- 150g pack ready-cooked mussels (not in shells)
- 60g peeled prawns
- large handful of parsley , chopped

Method

STEP 1

Heat the oil in a wide non-stick pan with a tight-fitting lid. Fry the onions and potatoes for about 5 mins, or until starting to soften. Add the peppers, courgettes, tomatoes and garlic, then stir in the vinegar, if using, the bouillon and 200ml water. Bring to a simmer, cover and cook for 25 mins, or until the peppers and courgettes are very tender (if your pan doesn't have a tight-fitting lid, wet a sheet of baking parchment and place over the stew before covering – this helps keep in the juices).

STEP 2

Add the hake fillets, mussels and prawns, then cover and cook for 5 mins more, or until the fish flakes easily when tested with a fork. Scatter over the parsley and serve.

Sugar-free lemon drizzle cake

Prep:10 mins **Cook:**1 hr - 1 hr and 10 mins

Cuts into 8-10 slices

Ingredients

- 225g self-raising flour, sifted
- ½ tsp baking powder
- 225g xylitol (see tip below)
- 2 lemons, zest only
- 2 large eggs, at room temperature
- 125ml sunflower oil
- 1 tbsp milk
- 200g 0% fat Greek yogurt

Drizzle

- 1 lemon, juice only
- 50g xylitol

Method

STEP 1

Preheat the oven to 180C/ 160C fan/ Gas 4. Grease and line a 1.2 litre loaf tin (22cm x 13cm width, 7cm depth) with baking parchment. Mix together the flour, baking powder, xylitol and lemon zest in a large bowl.

STEP 2

Mix the eggs, sunflower oil, milk and yoghurt together in a separate bowl or jug and stir them into the flour mixture.

STEP 3

Spoon into a tin and smooth the surface. Transfer to the oven immediately, bake on the middle shelf of the oven for 1 hour – 1 hour 10 mins. Check after 50 mins, if the cake is becoming too dark, cover loosely with foil.

STEP 4

Just before the end of cooking time, make the drizzle by heating the lemon juice and xylitol. Stir over a low heat until the xylitol has dissolved. Once the cake is cooked, take it out of the oven and pour over the drizzle.

STEP 5

Cool in the tin before turning it out.

Yakitori chicken

Prep:15 mins **Cook:**25 mins

Serves 4

Ingredients

- 100ml soy sauce

- 100ml mirin
- 50ml sake
- 2 tbsp caster sugar
- 500g boneless and skinless chicken thighs, chopped into 3cm chunks
- 4 spring onions , each cut into three

You will need

- 4 flat teppo gushi bamboo skewers

Method

STEP 1

Soak the skewers in a bowl of water while you prepare everything else, to prevent them from burning. Tip the soy, mirin, sake and sugar into a small saucepan, and cook over a medium heat for about 15 mins until the sauce is glossy.

STEP 2

Remove the skewers from the water and thread each one with a piece of chicken, followed by a piece of spring onion. Repeat twice more so the skewer is well stacked. Fill all four skewers.

STEP 3

Heat a large frying pan over a medium heat – you want to cook the chicken fairly gently so it soaks up the sauce. Put the skewers in the pan, then brush with the sauce. Cook for 10 mins, turning regularly and brushing in all the sauce. Serve immediately.

Herb & garlic pork with summer ratatouille

Prep:15 mins **Cook:**25 mins

4 (or 2 with leftovers for other meals)

Ingredients

- 2 tsp rapeseed oil
- 2 red onions , halved and sliced
- 2 peppers (any colour), diced
- 1 large aubergine , diced
- 2 large courgettes , halved and sliced

- 2 garlic cloves , chopped
- 400g can chopped tomatoes
- 2 tsp vegetable bouillon
- 1 thyme spig
- handful basil , stalks chopped, leaves torn and kept separate

For the pork

- 475g pork tenderloin, fat trimmed off, cut into 2 equal pieces
- 2 garlic cloves , crushed
- 1 tbsp thyme leaves , plus a few sprigs to decorate
- 1 tsp rapeseed oil
- brown rice or new potatoes, to serve

Method

STEP 1

Heat the oil in a large non-stick pan and fry the onions for 5 mins or until softened. Stir in the peppers, aubergine, courgettes and garlic, and cook, stirring, for a few mins. Tip in the tomatoes and 1 can of water, then stir in the bouillon, thyme and basil stalks. Cover and simmer for 20 mins or until tender. Stir through the basil leaves.

STEP 2

Meanwhile, rub the pork with the garlic, then scatter with the thyme and some black pepper, patting it so it sticks all over. Heat the oil in a non-stick frying pan and cook the pork for about 12 mins, turning frequently so it browns on all sides, until tender but still moist. Cover and rest for 5 mins.

STEP 3

If you're making this as part of the Healthy Diet Plan, set aside half of the pork to use in the curried pork bulghar salad later in the week and store in the fridge once cooled. Chill the half of the ratatouille and use it to make the ratatouille pasta salad with rocket for another day. If you are serving four you can skip this step.

STEP 4

To serve, slice the pork and serve with the ratatouille, some brown rice or new potatoes and some extra thyme.

Smashed chicken with corn slaw

Prep:10 mins **Cook:**5 mins

Serves 4

Ingredients

For the chicken

- 4 skinless chicken breast fillets
- 1 lime , zested and juiced
- 2 tbsp bio yogurt
- 1 tsp fresh thyme leaves
- ¼ tsp turmeric
- 2 tbsp finely chopped coriander
- 1 garlic clove , finely grated
- 1 tsp rapeseed oil

For the slaw

- 1 small avocado
- 1 lime , zested and juiced
- 2 tbsp bio yogurt
- 2 tbsp finely chopped coriander
- 160g corn , cut from 2 cobs
- 1 red pepper , deseeded and chopped
- 1 red onion , halved and finely sliced
- 320g white cabbage , finely sliced
- 150g new potatoes , boiled, to serve

Method

STEP 1

Cut the chicken breasts in half, then put them between two sheets of baking parchment and bash with a rolling pin to flatten. Mix the lime zest and juice with the yogurt, thyme, turmeric, coriander and garlic in a large bowl. Add the chicken and stir until well coated. Leave to marinate while you make the slaw.

STEP 2

Mash the avocado with the lime juice and zest, 2 tbsp yogurt and the coriander. Stir in the corn, red pepper, onion and cabbage.

STEP 3

Heat a large non-stick frying pan or griddle pan, then cook the chicken in batches for a few mins each side – they'll cook quickly as they're thin. Serve the hot chicken with the slaw and the new potatoes. If you're cooking for two, chill half the chicken and slaw for lunch another day (eat within two days).

Soup maker tomato soup

Prep:5 mins **Cook:**30 mins

Serves 2

Ingredients

- 500g ripe tomatoes , off the vine and quartered or halved
- 1 small onion , chopped
- ½ small carrot , chopped
- ½ celery stick, chopped
- 1 tsp tomato purée
- pinch of sugar
- 450ml vegetable stock

Method

STEP 1

Put all the ingredients into the soup maker and press the 'smooth soup' function. Make sure you don't fill the soup maker above the max fill line.

STEP 2

Once the cycle is complete, season well, and check the soup for sweetness. Add a little more sugar, salt or tomato puree for depth of colour, if you like.

Sweet potato jackets with guacamole & kidney beans

Prep:10 mins **Cook:**45 mins

Serves 2

Ingredients

- a drop of rapeseed oil
- 2 sweet potatoes
- 1 large avocado
- juice 1 lime, plus 2 wedges
- 1 red chilli, deseeded and finely chopped
- 2 tomatoes, finely chopped
- ⅓ small pack coriander, leaves roughly chopped
- 1 small red onion, finely chopped
- 400g can red kidney beans in water, drained

Method

STEP 1

Heat oven to 220C/200C fan/gas 7, oil the sweet potatoes, then put them straight on the oven shelf and roast for 45 mins or until tender all the way through when pierced with a knife.

STEP 2

Meanwhile, mash the avocado with the lime juice in a small bowl, then stir in the chilli, tomatoes, coriander and onion.

STEP 3

Cut the potatoes in half and top with the beans and guacamole. Serve with the lime wedges for squeezing over.

Thai chicken parcel with sugar snap peas & rice

Prep:10 mins **Cook:**20 mins

Serves 2

Ingredients

- 2 skinless chicken breasts
- small pack coriander , chopped
- 1 pak choi , quartered
- 175g sugar snap pea
- 1 tsp fish sauce
- 1 tsp soy sauce
- 2 tbsp rice vinegar
- 2 tbsp sweet chilli sauce
- zest and juice 1 lime
- 1 tbsp Thai green curry paste
- 100g basmati rice

Method

STEP 1

Heat oven to 220C/200C fan/gas 7. Heat a non-stick frying pan over a high heat and cook the chicken breasts for 4-5 mins on each side until browned.

STEP 2

Lay a large piece of baking parchment on a baking tray, add half the coriander, the pak choi and sugar snap peas, then place the chicken breasts on top. Combine the fish and soy sauce, rice vinegar, sweet chilli, lime zest and juice, and curry paste, and pour over the chicken and veg, then cover with another piece of parchment. Fold up each edge to form a parcel and cook for 12-15 mins.

STEP 3

Meanwhile, cook the rice following pack instructions. Remove the parcel from the oven, leave to sit for 1-2 mins, then cut open and add the rest of the coriander. Serve with the rice.

Leek, tomato & barley risotto with pan-cooked cod

Prep:10 mins **Cook:**20 mins

Serves 2

Ingredients

- 2 tsp rapeseed oil
- 1 large leek (315g), thinly sliced
- 2 garlic cloves , chopped
- 400g can barley (don't drain)
- 2 tsp vegetable bouillon
- 1 tsp finely chopped sage
- 1 tbsp thyme leaves , plus a few extra to serve
- 160g cherry tomatoes
- 50g finely grated parmesan
- 2 skin-on cod fillets or firm white fish fillets

Method

STEP 1

Heat 1 tsp oil in a non-stick pan and fry the leek and garlic for 5-10 mins, stirring frequently until softened, adding a splash of water to help it cook if you need to.

STEP 2

Tip in the barley with its liquid, then stir in the bouillon, sage and thyme. Simmer, stirring frequently for 3-4 mins. Add the tomatoes and cook about 4-5 mins more until they soften and start to split, adding a drop more water if necessary. Stir in the parmesan.

STEP 3

Meanwhile, heat the remaining oil in a non-stick pan and fry the cod, skin-side down, for 4-5 mins. Flip the fillets over to cook briefly on the other side. Spoon the risotto into two bowls. Serve the cod on top with a few thyme leaves, if you like.

Breakfast super-shake

Prep:5 mins no cook

Serves 1

Ingredients

- 100ml full-fat milk
- 2 tbsp natural yogurt
- 1 banana
- 150g frozen fruits of the forest
- 50g blueberries
- 1 tbsp chia seeds
- ½ tsp cinnamon
- 1 tbsp goji berries
- 1 tsp mixed seeds
- 1 tsp honey (ideally Manuka)

Method

STEP 1

Put the ingredients in a blender and blitz until smooth. Pour into a glass and enjoy!

Green minestrone with tortellini

Prep:5 mins **Cook:**25 mins

Serves 4

Ingredients

- 2 tbsp olive or rapeseed oil
- 1 onion , chopped
- 1 small leek , chopped
- 1 celery stick , chopped
- 3 garlic cloves , crushed
- 2 bay leaves
- 1l good-quality chicken or vegetable stock
- 100g shredded spring veg or cabbage
- 50g frozen peas
- 1 lemon , zested
- 250g tortellini

Method

STEP 1

Heat the olive or rapeseed oil in a large pan. Add the onion, leek and celery stick. Cook for 8-10 mins until softened, then stir in the garlic and bay leaves. Pour in the chicken or vegetable stock, then cover and simmer for 10 mins. Add the spring veg or cabbage, peas, lemon zest and tortellini (spinach tortellini works well). Cover and cook for another 3 mins, season well and ladle into bowls.

Baked piri-piri tilapia with crushed potatoes

Prep:10 mins **Cook:**25 mins

Serves 4

Ingredients

- 600g small new potatoes
- 2 red peppers, cut into chunky pieces
- 1 tbsp red wine vinegar
- drizzle of extra virgin olive oil
- 4 large pieces tilapia or cod
- green salad, to serve

For the piri-piri sauce

- 6 hot pickled peppers (I used Peppadew)
- 1 tsp chilli flakes
- 2 garlic cloves
- juice and zest 1 lemon
- 1 tbsp red wine vinegar
- 2 tbsp extra virgin olive oil
- 1 tbsp smoked paprika

Method

STEP 1

Heat oven to 220C/200C fan/gas 7. Boil the potatoes until knife-tender, then drain. Spread out on a large baking tray and gently crush with the back of a spatula. Add the peppers, drizzle with the vinegar and oil, season well and roast for 25 mins.

STEP 2

Put the piri-piri ingredients in a food processor with some salt. Purée until fine, then pour into a bowl. Put the fish on a baking tray and spoon over some of the piri-piri sauce. Season and bake for the final 10 mins of the potatoes' cooking time. Serve everything with the extra sauce and a green salad on the side.

All-in–one chicken with wilted spinach

Prep:20 mins **Cook:**1 hr

Serves 2

Ingredients

- 2 beetroot , peeled and cut into small chunks
- 300g celeriac , cut into small chunks
- 2 red onions , quartered
- 8 garlic cloves , 4 crushed, the rest left whole, but peeled
- 1 tbsp rapeseed oil
- 1½ tbsp fresh thyme leaves , plus extra to serve
- 1 lemon , zested and juiced
- 1 tsp fennel seeds
- 1 tsp English mustard powder
- 1 tsp smoked paprika
- 4 tbsp bio yogurt
- 4 bone-in chicken thighs , skin removed
- 260g bag spinach

Method

STEP 1

Heat oven to 200C/180C fan/gas 6. Tip the beetroot, celeriac, onions and whole garlic cloves into a shallow roasting tin. Add the oil, 1 tbsp thyme, half the lemon zest, fennel seeds and a squeeze of lemon juice, then toss together. Roast for 20 mins while you prepare the chicken.

STEP 2

Stir the mustard powder and paprika into 2 tbsp yogurt in a bowl. Add half the crushed garlic, the remaining lemon zest and thyme, and juice from half the lemon. Add the chicken and toss well until it's coated all over. Put the chicken in the tin with the veg and roast for 40 mins until the chicken is cooked through and the vegetables are tender.

STEP 3

About 5 mins before the chicken is ready, wash and drain the spinach and put it in a pan with the remaining crushed garlic. Cook until wilted, then turn off the heat and stir in the remaining yogurt. Scatter some extra thyme over the chicken and vegetables, then serve.

Apple & almond cake

Prep: 10 mins **Cook:** 35 mins - 40 mins

Serves 8

Ingredients

- 125ml (½ cup) olive oil
- 140g (½ cup) maple syrup or agave syrup
- 2 eggs
- 130g (1/2 cup) apple sauce (shop-bought or homemade)
- 185g (2 cups) ground almonds
- 1 tsp baking powder
- 1 tsp cinnamon

For the topping

- 1 apple , skin-on, cored and diced
- tiny splash olive oil
- 1 tbsp maple syrup
- ½ tsp cinnamon

Method

STEP 1

Heat oven to 190C/170C fan/gas 5, and lightly oil a 20cm springform tin and line the base with a circle of baking parchment.

STEP 2

In a stand mixer, or using a hand blender, whizz together the oil and maple syrup for 30 secs. Add the eggs and whizz for another 1 min before adding the apple sauce and blending for a further 30 secs. Tip in the ground almonds, baking powder, 1 tsp salt and cinnamon, blend for 30 secs and your batter is done. Pour it into the tin, and bake for around 30-40 mins or until the top is a deep golden brown, the cake is coming away from the sides a little, and a skewer inserted into the centre comes out clean.

STEP 3

While it's cooking, make the topping. In a small frying pan, cook the apple gently with the rest of the topping ingredients and ½ tsp salt until the apple is soft and gently caramelised. When the cake is ready, scatter the bronzed apple chunks on top of the cake. You could also make it with chunks of caramelised peach or plum on top, or some cherry compote, or any berries which you have softened in a pan with a little water and maple syrup. Eat warm, as a pudding, with a spoonful of Greek yogurt, or cold with a cup of tea or coffee.

Easy vegan pho

Prep:10 mins **Cook:**20 mins

Serves 2

Ingredients

- 100g rice noodles
- 1 tsp Marmite
- 1 tsp vegetable oil
- 50g chestnut mushrooms , sliced
- 1 leek , sliced
- 2 tbsp soy sauce

To serve

- 1 red chilli , sliced (deseeded if you don't like it too hot)
- ½ bunch mint , leaves picked and stalk discarded
- handful salted peanuts
- sriracha , to serve

Method

STEP 1

Tip the noodles into a bowl and cover with boiling water. Leave to stand for 10 mins, then drain, rinse in cold water and set aside.

STEP 2

In a jug, mix the Marmite with 500ml boiling water. Set aside while you cook the vegetables.

STEP 3

Heat the oil in a saucepan, then add the mushrooms and leek. Cook for 10-15 mins until softened and beginning to colour, then add the soy sauce and Marmite and water mixture and stir. Bring to the boil for 5 mins.

STEP 4

Divide the noodles between two deep bowls, then ladle over the hot broth. Top with the chilli slices, mint leaves and peanuts, and serve with some sriracha on the side.

Seared beef salad with capers & mint

Prep:10 mins **Cook:**12 mins

Serves 2

Ingredients

- 150g new potatoes , thickly sliced
- 160g fine green beans , trimmed and halved
- 160g frozen peas
- rapeseed oil , for brushing

- 200g lean fillet steak , trimmed of any fat
- 160g romaine lettuce , roughly torn into pieces

For the dressing

- 1 tbsp extra virgin olive oil
- 2 tsp cider vinegar
- ½ tsp English mustard powder
- 2 tbsp chopped mint
- 3 tbsp chopped basil
- 1 garlic clove , finely grated
- 1 tbsp capers

Method

STEP 1

Cook the potatoes in a pan of simmering water for 5 mins. Add the beans and cook 5 mins more, then tip in the peas and cook for 2 mins until all the vegetables are just tender. Drain.

STEP 2

Meanwhile, measure all the dressing ingredients in a large bowl and season with black pepper. Stir and crush the herbs and capers with the back of a spoon to intensify their flavours.

STEP 3

Brush a little oil over the steak and grind over some black pepper. Heat a non-stick frying pan over a high heat and cook the steak for 4 mins on one side and 2-3 mins on the other, depending on the thickness and how rare you like it. Transfer to a plate to rest while you carry on with the rest of the salad.

STEP 4

Mix the warm vegetables into the dressing until well coated, then add the lettuce and toss again. Pile onto plates. Slice the steak and turn in any dressing left in the bowl, add to the salad and serve while still warm.

Minty griddled chicken & peach salad

Prep:10 mins **Cook:**15 mins

Serves 2

Ingredients

- 1 lime , zested and juiced
- 1 tbsp rapeseed oil
- 2 tbsp mint , finely chopped, plus a few leaves to serve
- 1 garlic clove , finely grated
- 2 skinless chicken breast fillets (300g)
- 160g fine beans , trimmed and halved
- 2 peaches (200g), each cut into 8 thick wedges
- 1 red onion , cut into wedges
- 1 large Little Gem lettuce (165g), roughly shredded
- ½ x 60g pack rocket
- 1 small avocado , stoned and sliced
- 240g cooked new potatoes

Method

STEP 1

Mix the lime zest and juice, oil and mint, then put half in a bowl with the garlic. Thickly slice the chicken at a slight angle, add to the garlic mixture and toss together with plenty of black pepper.

STEP 2

Cook the beans in a pan of water for 3-4 mins until just tender. Meanwhile, griddle the chicken and onion for a few mins each side until cooked and tender. Transfer to a plate, then quickly griddle the peaches. If you don't have a griddle pan, use a non-stick frying pan with a drop of oil.

STEP 3

Toss the warm beans and onion in the remaining mint mixture, and pile onto a platter or into individual shallow bowls with the lettuce and rocket. Top with the avocado, peaches and chicken and scatter over the mint. Serve with the potatoes while still warm.

Parma pork with potato salad

Prep:15 mins **Cook:**15 mins

Serves 2

Ingredients

- 175g new potatoes (we used Jersey Royals), scrubbed and thickly sliced
- 3 celery sticks, thickly sliced
- 3 tbsp bio yogurt
- 2 gherkins (about 85g each), sliced
- ¼ tsp caraway seeds
- ½ tsp Dijon mustard
- 2 x 100g pieces lean pork tenderloin
- 2 tsp chopped sage
- 2 slices Parma ham
- 1 tsp rapeseed oil
- 2 tsp balsamic vinegar
- 2 handfuls salad leaves

Method

STEP 1

Bring a pan of water to the boil, add the potatoes and celery and cook for 8 mins. Meanwhile, mix the yogurt, guerkins, caraway and mustard in a bowl. When the potatoes and celery are cooked, drain and set aside for a few mins to cool a little.

STEP 2

Bash the pork pieces with a rolling pin to flatten them. Sprinkle over the sage and some pepper, then top each with a slice of Parma ham. Heat the oil in a non-stick pan, add the pork and cook for a couple of mins each side, turning carefully. Add the balsamic vinegar and let it sizzle in the pan.

STEP 3

Stir the potatoes and celery into the dressing and serve with the pork, with some salad leaves on the side.

Yaki udon

Prep: 10 mins **Cook:** 5 mins

Serves 2

Ingredients

- 250g dried udon noodles (400g frozen or fresh)
- 2 tbsp sesame oil
- 1 onion, thickly sliced
- ¼ head white cabbage, roughly sliced
- 10 shiitake mushrooms
- 4 spring onions, finely sliced

For the sauce

- 4 tbsp mirin
- 2 tbsp soy sauce
- 1 tbsp caster sugar
- 1 tbsp Worcestershire sauce (or vegetarian alternative)

Method

STEP 1

Boil some water in a large saucepan. Add 250ml cold water and the udon noodles. (As they are so thick, adding cold water helps them to cook a little bit slower so the middle cooks through). If using frozen or fresh noodles, cook for 2 mins or until al dente; dried will take longer, about 5-6 mins. Drain and leave in the colander.

STEP 2

Heat 1 tbsp of the oil, add the onion and cabbage and sauté for 5 mins until softened. Add the mushrooms and some spring onions, and sauté for 1 more min. Pour in the remaining sesame oil and the noodles. If using cold noodles, let them heat through before adding the ingredients for the sauce – otherwise tip in straight away and keep stir-frying until sticky and piping hot. Sprinkle with the remaining spring onions.

Mushroom & potato soup

Prep:15 mins **Cook:**30 mins

Serves 4

Ingredients

- 1 tbsp rapeseed oil
- 2 large onions , halved and thinly sliced
- 20g dried porcini mushrooms
- 3 tsp vegetable bouillon powder
- 300g chestnut mushrooms , chopped
- 3 garlic cloves , finely grated
- 300g potato , finely diced
- 2 tsp fresh thyme
- 4 carrots , finely diced
- 2 tbsp chopped parsley
- 8 tbsp bio yogurt
- 55g walnut pieces

Method

STEP 1

Heat the oil in a large pan. Tip in the onions and fry for 10 mins until golden. Meanwhile, pour 1.2 litres boiling water over the dried mushrooms and stir in the bouillon.

STEP 2

Add the fresh mushrooms and garlic to the pan with the potatoes, thyme and carrots, and continue to fry until the mushrooms soften and start to brown.

STEP 3

Pour in the dried mushrooms and stock, cover the pan and leave to simmer for 20 mins. Stir in the parsley and plenty of pepper. Ladle into bowls and serve each portion topped with 2 tbsp yogurt and a quarter of the walnuts. The rest can be chilled and reheated the next day.

Coconut crêpes with raspberry sauce

Prep:10 mins **Cook:**25 mins

Serves 6

Ingredients

For the raspberry sauce

- 200g raspberries
- 2 tsp cornflour
- 2 tsp maple syrup

For the coconut crêpes

- 140g plain flour
- 2 large eggs
- 300ml coconut milk
- 2 tbsp toasted desiccated coconut
- a little sunflower oil , for frying

Method

STEP 1

Set aside 6 of the raspberries. Mix the cornflour with 1 tbsp water until smooth. Measure 300ml water in a pan, and stir in the cornflour paste. Heat, stirring, until thickened. Add the remaining raspberries and cook gently, mashing the berries to a pulp. Strain the mixture through a sieve into a bowl to remove the seeds, pushing through as much of the mixture as you can. Quarter the reserved raspberries and add to the sauce, along with the maple syrup.

STEP 2

To make the crêpes, tip the flour and a pinch of salt into a large jug, then beat in the eggs, coconut milk, 200ml water and 11/2 tbsp toasted coconut to make a batter the consistency of double cream. Thin with a little more water if it is too thick. Heat a small frying pan with a dash of oil, then pour in a little batter, swirling the pan so that it completely covers the base. Leave to set over the heat for 1 min, then carefully flip it over and cook the other side for a few secs more. Transfer to a plate and repeat with the remaining batter until you have at least 12. Stir the batter to redistribute the coconut as you use it. Serve 2 crêpes per person with a drizzle of the sauce and a little of the remaining toasted coconut.

Low-fat cherry cheesecake

Prep:1 hr **Cook:**30 mins Plus overnight chilling

Cuts into 8 slices

Ingredients

- 25g butter , melted
- 140g amaretti biscuit , crushed
- 3 sheets leaf gelatine
- zest and juice 1 orange
- 2 x 250g tubs quark
- 250g tub ricotta
- 2 tsp vanilla extract
- 100g icing sugar
- For the topping
- 400g fresh cherry , stoned
- 5 tbsp cherry jam
- 1 tbsp cornflour

Method

STEP 1

Line the sides of a 20cm round loose-bottomed cake tin with baking parchment. Stir the butter into twothirds of the biscuit crumbs, and reserve the rest. Sprinkle the buttery crumbs over the base of the tin and press down. Soak the gelatine in cold water for 5-10 mins until soft.

STEP 2

Warm the orange juice in a small pan or the microwave until almost boiling. Squeeze the gelatine of excess water, then stir into the juice to dissolve.

STEP 3

Beat the quark, ricotta, vanilla and icing sugar together with an electric whisk until really smooth. Then, with the beaters still running, pour in the juice mixture and beat to combine. Pour the cheesecake mixture over the crumbs and smooth the top. Cover with cling film and chill overnight.

STEP 4

To make the topping, put the cherries in a pan with the orange zest and 100ml water. Cook, covered, for 15 mins until the cherries are softened. Put one-third of the cherries in a bowl and mash with a potato masher to give you a chunky compote. Return to the pan, add the jam, cornflour and 2 tbsp water, and mix to combine. Cook until thickened and saucy – if the sauce is too dry, add a splash more water. Cool to room temperature.

STEP 5

Just before serving, carefully remove the cheesecake from the tin and peel off the parchment. Scatter over the remaining biscuit crumbs and some cherry sauce. Serve in slices with the remaining cherry sauce alongside.

Jam turnovers

Prep:10 mins **Cook:**20 mins

Serves 6

Ingredients

- 320g sheet puff pastry
- 1 heaped tbsp jam (apricot, raspberry or strawberry work well)
- 1 beaten egg
- icing sugar , for dusting
- clotted cream , to serve

Method

STEP 1

Heat the oven to 200C/180C fan/gas 6. Unravel the puff pastry on a lightly floured surface. Cut the pastry into six squares. Spoon the jam in the centre of each pastry square. Seal the edges by pressing down with a fork and brush with the egg. Lay on a lined baking sheet and bake for 20 mins. Dust with the icing sugar and serve with the clotted cream.

Veggie okonomiyaki

Prep:15 mins **Cook:**10 mins

Serves 2

Ingredients

- 3 large eggs
- 50g plain flour
- 50ml milk
- 4 spring onions , trimmed and sliced
- 1 pak choi , sliced
- 200g Savoy cabbage , shredded
- 1 red chilli , deseeded and finely chopped, plus extra to serve
- ½ tbsp low-salt soy sauce
- ½ tbsp rapeseed oil
- 1 heaped tbsp low-fat mayonnaise
- ½ lime , juiced
- sushi ginger , to serve (optional)
- wasabi , to serve (optional)

Method

STEP 1

Whisk together the eggs, flour and milk until smooth. Add half the spring onions, the pak choi, cabbage, chilli and soy sauce. Heat the oil in a small frying pan and pour in the batter. Cook, covered, over a medium heat for 7-8 mins. Flip the okonomiyaki into a second frying pan, then return it to the heat and cook for a further 7-8 mins until a skewer inserted into it comes out clean.

STEP 2

Mix the mayonnaise and lime juice together in a small bowl. Transfer the okonomiyaki to a plate, then drizzle over the lime mayo and top with the extra chilli and spring onion and the sushi ginger, if using. Serve with the wasabi on the side, if you like.

Easy chicken stew

Prep:10 mins **Cook:**50 mins

Serves 4

Ingredients

- 1 tbsp olive oil
- 1 bunch spring onions , sliced, white and green parts separated
- 1 small swede (350g), peeled and chopped into small pieces
- 400g potatoes , peeled and chopped into small pieces
- 8 skinless boneless chicken thighs
- 1 tbsp Dijon mustard
- 500ml chicken stock
- 200g Savoy cabbage or spring cabbage, sliced
- 2 tsp cornflour (optional)
- crusty bread or cheese scones, to serve (optional)

Method

STEP 1

Heat the oil in a large saucepan. Add the white spring onion slices and fry for 1 min to soften. Tip in the swede and potatoes and cook for 2-3 mins more, then add the chicken, mustard and stock. Cover and cook for 35 mins, or until the vegetables are tender and the chicken cooked through.

STEP 2

Add the cabbage and simmer for another 5 mins. If the stew looks too thin, mix the cornflour with 1 tbsp cold water and pour a couple of teaspoonfuls into the pan; let the stew bubble and thicken, then check again. If it's still too thin, add a little more of the cornflour mix and let the stew bubble and thicken some more.

STEP 3

Season to taste, then spoon the stew into deep bowls. Scatter over the green spring onion slices and serve with crusty bread or warm cheese scones, if you like.

Last-minute Christmas loaf cake

Prep:25 mins **Cook:**1 hr and 15 mins Plus 2 hrs soaking

Serves 10

Ingredients

- 200g raisins and sultanas
- 50g sour cherries
- 100g dried figs , chopped
- 150g mixed peel
- 1 orange , zested and juiced
- 250ml brandy
- 115g butter , plus extra melted for the tin
- 115g muscovado sugar
- 4 eggs , beaten
- 120g self-raising flour
- 1 tsp baking powder
- 60g brioche crumbs
- 40g chopped pecans and pistachios
- ½ tsp ground mace
- ½ tsp ground cinnamon
- icing sugar , to serve (optional)

Method

STEP 1

Tip the fruit and peel into a bowl with the orange juice and zest and 150ml of the brandy. Stir well, then leave in a warm place for 2 hrs for the fruit to plump up.

STEP 2

Heat oven to 170C/150C fan/gas 4. Brush a 900g loaf tin with the melted butter, then line with baking parchment. Beat the muscovado sugar and butter until light and fluffy, then add the eggs one at a time. Mix in the fruit and the rest of the ingredients except for the remaining brandy and icing sugar. Spoon the mixture into the loaf tin, put the tin in a deep tray and bake for 1 hr 15 mins-1 hr 30 mins or until a skewer prodded in comes out clean. Remove from the oven and immediately pour over the brandy (this makes it easier for the cake to soak it up). Leave to cool, then dust with icing sugar, if using.

Green chowder with prawns

Prep:10 mins **Cook:**20 mins - 30 mins

Serves 4

Ingredients

- 1 tbsp olive oil
- 1 onion , finely chopped
- 1 celery stick , finely chopped
- 1 garlic clove
- 300g petit pois
- 200g pack sliced kale
- 2 potatoes , finely chopped
- 1 low-salt chicken stock cube (we used Kallo)
- 100g cooked North Atlantic prawns

Method

STEP 1

Heat the oil in a saucepan over a medium heat. Add the onion and celery and cook for 5-6 mins until softened but not coloured. Add the garlic and cook for a further min. Stir in the petit pois, kale and potatoes, then add the stock cube and 750ml water. Bring to the boil and simmer for 10-12 mins until the potatoes are soft.

STEP 2

Tip ¾ of the mixture into a food processor and whizz until smooth. Add a little more water or stock if it's too thick. Pour the mixture back into the pan and add half the prawns.

STEP 3

Divide between four bowls and spoon the remaining prawns on top. Can be frozen for up to a month. Add the prawns once defrosted.

Mushroom brunch

Prep:5 mins **Cook:**12 mins - 15 mins

Serves 4

Ingredients

- 250g mushrooms
- 1 garlic clove

- 1 tbsp olive oil
- 160g bag kale
- 4 eggs

Method

STEP 1

Slice the mushrooms and crush the garlic clove. Heat the olive oil in a large non-stick frying pan, then fry the garlic over a low heat for 1 min. Add the mushrooms and cook until soft. Then, add the kale. If the kale won't all fit in the pan, add half and stir until wilted, then add the rest. Once all the kale is wilted, season.

STEP 2

Now crack in the eggs and keep them cooking gently for 2-3 mins. Then, cover with the lid to for a further 2-3 mins or until the eggs are cooked to your liking. Serve with bread.

Caipiroska

Prep:5 mins **Serves 1**

Ingredients

- 1 lime
- 2 tsp golden granulated sugar
- 50ml vodka
- crushed ice

Method

STEP 1

Cut the lime into small chunks, then put it into the bottom of a sturdy tumbler and add the golden granulated sugar. Crush really well with a muddler – you can also do this with a pestle and mortar.

STEP 2

Top up the tumbler with crushed ice, then add the vodka. Stir well to mix all the ingredients together, and serve.

Thai fried prawn & pineapple rice

Prep:10 mins **Cook:**15 mins

Serves 4

Ingredients

- 2 tsp sunflower oil
- bunch spring onions , greens and whites separated, both sliced
- 1 green pepper , deseeded and chopped into small chunks
- 140g pineapple , chopped into bite-sized chunks
- 3 tbsp Thai green curry paste
- 4 tsp light soy sauce , plus extra to serve
- 300g cooked basmati rice (brown, white or a mix - about 140g uncooked rice)
- 2 large eggs , beaten
- 140g frozen peas
- 225g can bamboo shoots , drained
- 250g frozen prawns , cooked or raw
- 2-3 limes , 1 juiced, the rest cut into wedges to serve
- handful coriander leaves (optional)

Method

STEP 1

Heat the oil in a wok or non-stick frying pan and fry the spring onion whites for 2 mins until softened. Stir in the pepper for 1 min, followed by the pineapple for 1 min more, then stir in the green curry paste and soy sauce.

STEP 2

Add the rice, stir-frying until piping hot, then push the rice to one side of the pan and scramble the eggs on the other side. Stir the peas, bamboo shoots and prawns into the rice and eggs, then heat through for 2 mins until the prawns are hot and the peas tender. Finally, stir in the spring onion greens, lime juice and coriander, if using. Spoon into bowls and serve with extra lime wedges and soy sauce.

Feta & clementine lunch bowl

Prep:15 mins **Cook:**15 mins

Serves 2

Ingredients

- 1 red onion , halved and thinly sliced
- 1 lemon , zested and juiced
- 2 clementines , 1 zested, flesh sliced
- 2 garlic cloves , chopped
- 400g can green lentils , drained
- 1 tbsp balsamic vinegar
- 1 ½ tbsp rapeseed oil
- 1 red pepper , quartered and sliced
- 60g feta , crumbled
- small handful mint , chopped
- 4 walnut halves , chopped

Method

STEP 1

Mix the onion with the lemon juice, lemon and clementine zest and garlic.

STEP 2

Tip the lentils into two bowls or lunchboxes and drizzle over the balsamic and 1 tbsp oil. Heat the remaining oil in a large non-stick wok, add the pepper and stir-fry for 3 mins. Tip in half the onion and cook until tender. Pile on top of the lentils, then mix the clementines, remaining onions, feta, mint and walnut pieces.

Carrot & ginger soup

Prep:15 mins **Cook:**25 mins - 30 mins

Serves 4

Ingredients

- 1 tbsp rapeseed oil
- 1 large onion, chopped

- 2 tbsp coarsely grated ginger
- 2 garlic cloves, sliced
- ½ tsp ground nutmeg
- 850ml vegetable stock
- 500g carrot (preferably organic), sliced
- 400g can cannellini beans (no need to drain)

Supercharged topping

- 4 tbsp almonds in their skins, cut into slivers
- sprinkle of nutmeg

Method

STEP 1

Heat the oil in a large pan, add the onion, ginger and garlic, and fry for 5 mins until starting to soften. Stir in the nutmeg and cook for 1 min more.

STEP 2

Pour in the stock, add the carrots, beans and their liquid, then cover and simmer for 20-25 mins until the carrots are tender.

STEP 3

Scoop a third of the mixture into a bowl and blitz the remainder with a hand blender or in a food processor until smooth. Return everything to the pan and heat until bubbling. Serve topped with the almonds and nutmeg.

French toast bacon butties

Prep:5 mins **Cook:**25 mins

Serves 2

Ingredients

- 2 eggs
- 180ml milk
- 1 tbsp caster sugar

- 4 slices white bread
- 2 tbsp butter
- 4 rashers back bacon, grilled
- icing sugar and syrup of choice (we like date syrup), to serve

Method

STEP 1

Whisk the eggs and milk with the sugar in a bowl. Soak the white sliced bread in the mixture.

STEP 2

Heat 1 tbsp of the butter in a non-stick frying pan and fry two slices of the soaked bread on a low–medium heat until golden and crisp, about 3–4 mins on each side. Remove from the pan and sandwich 2 slices of bacon between the slices of French toast. Repeat with the remaining soaked bread to make the other sandwich.

STEP 3

Serve with a dusting of icing sugar and a drizzle of syrup.

Miso mushroom & tofu noodle soup

Prep:10 mins **Cook:**15 mins

Serves 1

Ingredients

- 1 tbsp rapeseed oil
- 70g mixed mushrooms , sliced
- 50g smoked tofu , cut into small cubes
- ½ tbsp brown rice miso paste
- 50g dried buckwheat or egg noodles
- 2 spring onions , shredded

Method

STEP 1

Heat half the oil in a frying pan over a medium heat. Add the mushrooms and fry for 5-6 mins, or until golden. Transfer to a bowl using a slotted spoon and set aside. Add the remaining oil to the pan and fry the tofu for 3-4 mins, or until evenly golden.

STEP 2

Mix the miso paste with 325ml boiling water in a jug. Cook the noodles following pack instructions, then drain and transfer to a bowl. Top with the mushrooms and tofu, then pour over the miso broth. Scatter over the spring onions just before serving.

Sausage & butternut squash shells

Prep:15 mins **Cook:**35 mins

Serves 4

Ingredients

- 1 medium butternut squash , peeled and cut into medium chunks
- 1 ½ tbsp olive oil
- 2 garlic cloves , crushed
- 1 fennel bulb , thinly sliced (keep the green fronds to serve)
- 4 spring onions , thinly sliced
- 2 tsp chilli flakes
- 1 tsp fennel seeds
- 300g large pasta shells
- 3 pork sausages

Method

STEP 1

Put the squash in a microwaveable bowl with a splash of water. Cover with cling film and cook on high for 10 mins until soft. Tip into a blender.

STEP 2

Meanwhile, put a frying pan over a medium heat and pour in 1 tbsp olive oil. Add the garlic, sliced fennel, spring onions, half the chilli flakes, half the fennel seeds and a splash of water. Cook, stirring occasionally, for 5 mins until softened. Scrape into the blender with squash. Blitz to a smooth sauce, adding enough water to get to a creamy consistency. Season to taste.

STEP 3

Bring a pan of water to the boil and cook the pasta for 1 min less than the pack instructions. Put the frying pan back on the heat (don't bother washing it first – it's all flavour). Pour in the remaining oil, squeeze the sausagemeat from the skins into the pan and add the remaining chilli and remaining fennel seeds. Fry until browned and crisp, breaking down the sausagemeat with a spoon.

STEP 4

Drain the pasta and return to its pan on the heat. Pour in the butternut sauce and give everything a good mix to warm the sauce through. Divide between bowls and top with the crispy sausage mix and fennel fronds.

Mexican egg roll

Prep:5 mins **Cook:**10 mins

Serves 2

Ingredients

- 1 large egg
- a little rapeseed oil for frying
- 2 tbsp tomato salsa
- about 1 tbsp fresh coriander

Method

STEP 1

Beat the egg with 1 tbsp water. Heat the oil in a medium non-stick pan. Add the egg and swirl round the base of the pan, as though you are making a pancake, and cook until set. There is no need to turn it.

STEP 2

Carefully tip the pancake onto a board, spread with the salsa, sprinkle with the coriander, then roll it up. It can be eaten warm or cold – you can keep it for 2 days in the fridge.

Miso aubergines

Prep:5 mins **Cook:**50 mins

Serves 2

Ingredients

- 2 small aubergines, halved
- vegetable oil, for roasting and frying
- 50g brown miso
- 100g giant couscous
- 1 red chilli, thinly sliced
- ½ small pack coriander, leaves chopped

Method

STEP 1

Heat oven to 180C/160C fan/ gas 4. With a sharp knife, criss-cross the flesh of the aubergines in a diagonal pattern, then place on a baking tray. Brush the flesh with 1 tbsp vegetable oil.

STEP 2

Mix the miso with 25ml water to make a thick paste. Spread the paste over the aubergines, then cover the tray with foil and roast in the centre of the oven for 30 mins.

STEP 3

Remove the foil and roast the aubergines for a further 15-20 mins, depending on their size, until tender.

STEP 4

Meanwhile, bring a saucepan of salted water to the boil and heat 1 /2 tbsp vegetable oil over a medium-high heat in a frying pan. Add the couscous to the frying pan, toast for 2 mins until golden brown, then tip into the pan of boiling water and cook for 8-10 mins until tender (or following pack instructions). Drain well. Serve the aubergines with the couscous, topped with the chilli and a scattering of coriander leaves.

Sesame salmon, purple sprouting broccoli & sweet potato mash

Prep:10 mins **Cook:**15 mins

Serves 2

Ingredients

- 1 ½ tbsp sesame oil
- 1 tbsp low-salt soy sauce
- thumb-sized piece ginger, grated
- 1 garlic clove, crushed
- 1 tsp honey
- 2 sweet potatoes, scrubbed and cut into wedges
- 1 lime, cut into wedges
- 2 boneless skinless salmon fillets
- 250g purple sprouting broccoli
- 1 tbsp sesame seeds
- 1 red chilli, thinly sliced (deseeded if you don't like it too hot)

Method

STEP 1

Heat oven to 200C/180 fan/ gas 6 and line a baking tray with parchment. Mix together 1/2 tbsp sesame oil, the soy, ginger, garlic and honey. Put the sweet potato wedges, skin and all, into a glass bowl with the lime wedges. Cover with cling film and microwave on high for 12-14 mins until completely soft.

STEP 2

Meanwhile, spread the broccoli and salmon out on the baking tray. Spoon over the marinade and season. Roast in the oven for 10-12 mins, then sprinkle over the sesame seeds.

STEP 3

Remove the lime wedges and roughly mash the sweet potato using a fork. Mix in the remaining sesame oil, the chilli and some seasoning. Divide between plates, along with the salmon and broccoli.

Sweet & sour chicken adobo

Prep:20 mins **Cook:**6 hrs and 20 mins in a slow cooker (2 hrs 20 mins on the hob)

Serves 4

Ingredients

- 4 tbsp vegetable oil
- 600g skinless boneless chicken thighs , cut in half
- 2 tbsp cornflour , plus 1-2 tsp extra (optional)
- 1 large onion , cut into chunky pieces
- 5 garlic cloves , crushed
- 2 red peppers , deseeded and cut into chunky pieces
- 400ml can coconut milk
- 100ml low-salt soy sauce
- 100ml white wine vinegar
- 50g soft light brown sugar
- 6 bay leaves
- cooked basmati rice or brown rice, to serve

Method

STEP 1

Heat half the oil in a large pan. Put the chicken in a large bowl, season well and toss through the cornflour, then cook in batches until browned all over (don't overcrowd the pan or the chicken won't brown). Tip each batch straight into the slow cooker as you go, adding a little more oil to the pan if you need to. Add the onion, garlic and peppers, cook for a few mins to just soften, then add these to the slow cooker too.

STEP 2

If there is any cornflour remaining in the bowl, add a drop of the coconut milk and swirl it around, then pour into the slow cooker. Add the remaining coconut milk, the soy sauce, vinegar, sugar and bay leaves, season with plenty of black pepper, then heat the slow cooker to Low, cover with the lid and cook for 5-6 hrs until the meat is tender and the sauce has thickened. (If you don't have a slow cooker, tip the ingredients back into the pan, cover and cook for 11/2-2 hrs, stirring every now and then to prevent it from catching, and adding a splash of water if the stew looks dry.) If the sauce in the slow cooker is too thin, thicken it with the remaining cornflour. Mix 1-2 tsp cornflour with 1-2 tsp cold water to make a paste, ladle 2-3 spoonfuls of the sauce into a saucepan and bring to says a simmer, then stir in the cornflour paste and cook for 1-2 mins to thicken. Stir back into the slow cooker and cook on High for 10 mins more. Serve with rice and stir-fried veg.

Watermelon lollies

Prep:15 mins Plus at least 4 hours freezing

Serves 6 - 8

Ingredients

- 1 small watermelon
- 3 kiwis

Method

STEP 1

Halve 1 small watermelon and scoop the flesh out of one half into a bowl (you need about 375-400g). Pick out any black seeds. Purée the flesh using a hand blender or in a liquidiser. Fill ice lolly moulds three-quarters full with the purée, push the sticks in if you are using them, and freeze for at least 3 hrs, or overnight. Tip any remaining purée into an ice cube tray and freeze it.

STEP 2

Peel 3 kiwis and cut the green flesh away from the white core, discarding the core. Purée the flesh. Add a layer of about 4-5mm to the top of each lolly and refreeze for 1 hr. Add some green food colouring to the rest of the purée to darken it to the same colour as the watermelon rind. Pour a very thin layer onto the top of each lolly and freeze until you want to eat them.

Lamb dopiaza with broccoli rice

Prep:20 mins **Cook:**1 hr and 30 mins

Serves 2

Ingredients

- 225g lamb leg steaks , trimmed of excess fat and cut into 2.5cm/ 1in chunks

- 50g full-fat natural bio yogurt , plus 4 tbsp to serve
- 1 tbsp medium curry powder
- 2 tsp cold-pressed rapeseed oil
- 2 medium onions , 1 thinly sliced, 1 cut into 5 wedges
- 2 garlic cloves , peeled and finely sliced
- 1 tbsp ginger , peeled and finely chopped
- 1 small red chilli , finely chopped (deseeded if you don't like it too hot)
- 200g tomatoes , roughly chopped
- 50g dried split red lentils , rinsed
- 1/2 small pack of coriander , roughly chopped, plus extra to garnish
- 100g pack baby leaf spinach

For the broccoli rice

- 100g wholegrain brown rice
- 100g small broccoli florets

Method

STEP 1

Put the lamb in a large bowl and season well with ground black pepper. Add the yogurt and 1/2 tbsp of the curry powder, and stir well to combine.

STEP 2

Heat half the oil in a large non-stick saucepan. Fry the onion wedges over a high heat for 4-5 mins or until lightly browned and just tender. Tip onto a plate, set aside and return the pan to the heat.

STEP 3

Add the remaining oil, the sliced onions, garlic, ginger and chilli, cover and cook for 10 mins or until very soft, stirring occasionally. Remove the lid, increase the heat and cook for 2-3 mins more or until the onions are tinged with brown – this will add lots of flavour, but make sure they don't get burnt.

STEP 4

Reduce the heat once more and stir in the tomatoes and remaining curry powder. Cook for 1 min, then stir the lamb and yogurt into the pan and cook over a medium-high heat for 4-5 mins, stirring regularly.

STEP 5

Pour 300ml cold water into the pan, stir in the lentils and coriander, cover with a lid and leave to cook over a low heat for 45 mins – the sauce should be simmering gently and you can add a splash of water if the curry gets a little dry. Remove the lid every 10-15 mins and stir the curry.

STEP 6

With half an hour of the curry cooking time remaining, cook the rice in plenty of boiling water for 25 mins or until just tender. Add the broccoli florets and cook for a further 3 mins. Drain well.

STEP 7

Remove the lid from the curry, add the reserved onion wedges and continue to simmer over a high heat for a further 15 mins or until the lamb is tender, stirring regularly. Just before serving, stir in the spinach, a handful at a time, and let it wilt. Serve with the yogurt, coriander and broccoli rice.

Chargrilled chicken & kale Caesar salad

Prep:20 mins **Cook:**20 mins

Serves 4

Ingredients

- 1 anchovy
- 1 garlic clove
- 1 tsp Dijon mustard
- 100ml buttermilk
- 1 lemon , zested and juiced
- 200g bag kale , large tough stalks removed
- 200g defrosted frozen peas
- 6 skinless and boneless chicken thighs
- 2 thick slices crusty bread

- 3 tbsp cold pressed rapeseed oil
- 400g long-stem broccoli , cut in half lengthways
- 30g parmesan

Method

STEP 1

Mash the anchovy and garlic together using a pestle and mortar, then tip the mixture into a bowl and whisk in the mustard, buttermilk, lemon zest and juice, and season with black pepper. Put the kale and peas in a large bowl, pour over ¾ of the dressing, then massage into the kale so each leaf is coated.

STEP 2

Put the chicken thighs between two pieces of baking parchment, then bash out with a rolling pin to 1cm thickness.

STEP 3

Heat a griddle pan until searing hot. Brush the bread slices with a little oil, then griddle until lightly charred on all sides. Set aside.

STEP 4

Next, season the broccoli and brush the cut side of each piece with a little oil. Griddle, cut-side down, in batches for 3-4 mins until tender. Lastly, brush the remaining oil over the chicken thighs and season, then griddle the chicken for 3-4 mins on each side until cooked through.

STEP 5

Distribute the kale between four plates. Slice the chicken diagonally and break the bread into pieces. Top each of the plates with ¼ of the chicken, broccoli and croutons. Grate over the parmesan in large shavings and drizzle with the remaining dressing to serve.

Slow cooker Turkish breakfast eggs

Prep:15 mins **Cook:**5 hrs - 6 hrs

Serves 4

Ingredients

- 1 tbsp olive oil
- 2 onions , finely sliced
- 1 red pepper , cored and finely sliced
- 1 small red chilli , finely sliced
- 8 cherry tomatoes
- 1 slice sourdough bread , cubed
- 4 eggs
- 2 tbsp skimmed milk
- small bunch parsley , finely chopped
- 4 tbsp natural yogurt , to serve

Method

STEP 1

Oil the inside of a small slow cooker and heat if necessary. Heat the remaining oil in a heavy-based frying pan. Stir in the onions, pepper and chilli. Cook until they begin to soften. Tip into the slow cooker and add the cherry tomatoes and bread and stir everything. Season.

STEP 2

Whisk the eggs with the milk and parsley and pour this over the top, making sure all the other ingredients are covered. Cook for 5-6 hours. Serve with the yogurt.

Prawn fried rice

Prep:5 mins **Cook:**25 mins

Serves 4

Ingredients

- 250g long-grain brown rice
- 150g frozen peas
- 100g mangetout
- 1½ tbsp rapeseed oil
- 1 onion , finely chopped
- 2 garlic cloves , crushed
- thumb-sized piece of ginger , finely grated

- 150g raw king prawns
- 3 medium eggs , beaten
- 2 tsp sesame seeds
- 1 tbsp low-salt soy sauce
- ½ tbsp rice or white wine vinegar
- 4 spring onions , trimmed and sliced

Method

STEP 1

Cook the rice following pack instructions. Boil a separate pan of water and blanch the peas and mangetout for 1 min, then drain and set aside with the rice.

STEP 2

Meanwhile, heat the oil in a large non-stick frying pan or wok over a medium heat and fry the onion for 10 mins or until golden brown. Add the garlic and ginger and fry for a further minute. Tip in the blanched vegetables and fry for 5 mins, then the prawns and fry for a further 2 mins. Stir the rice into the pan then push everything to one side. Pour the beaten eggs into the empty side of the pan and stir to scramble them. Fold everything together with the sesame seeds, soy and vinegar, then finish with the spring onions scattered over.

Ham & piccalilli salad

Prep:15 mins No cook

Serves 4

Ingredients

- 4 tbsp piccalilli
- 3 tbsp natural yogurt
- 12 silverskin pickled onions , halved
- 130g pea shoots
- 180g pulled ham hock or shredded cooked ham
- ½ cucumber , halved and thickly sliced
- 100g fresh peas
- 40g mature cheddar , shaved
- crusty bread , to serve

Method

STEP 1

Mix the piccalilli, yogurt, onions and 4 tbsp water together to make a dressing. Season and set aside.

STEP 2

Toss the pea shoots, ham, cucumber and peas together. Pile onto a serving plate, then drizzle over the dressing. Top with the cheese and serve with crusty bread.

Avocado & bean triangles

Prep:5 mins No cook

Serves 2

Ingredients

- 3 triangluar bread thins
- 210g can red kidney beans , drained
- 1 tbsp finely chopped dill , plus extra for garnish
- 1/2 lemon , for squeezing
- 1 tomato , chopped
- 1 small avocado
- 1 small red onion , finely chopped

Method

STEP 1

Follow our triangular bread thins recipe to make your own. While they bake, roughly mash the beans with the dill and a good squeeze of lemon then stir in the tomato.

STEP 2

Cut the bread triangles in half and top with the beans. Scoop the avocado into a bowl and roughly mash with a squeeze more lemon. Spoon the avocado onto the beans, scatter over the chopped onion, then garnish with the remaining dill.

Summer carrot, tarragon & white bean soup

Prep:10 mins **Cook:**20 mins

Serves 4

Ingredients

- 1 tbsp rapeseed oil
- 2 large leeks , well washed, halved lengthways and finely sliced
- 700g carrots , chopped
- 1.4l hot reduced-salt vegetable bouillon (we used Marigold)
- 4 garlic cloves , finely grated
- 2 x 400g cans cannellini beans in water
- ⅔ small pack tarragon , leaves roughly chopped

Method

STEP 1

Heat the oil over a medium heat in a large pan and fry the leeks and carrots for 5 mins to soften.

STEP 2

Pour over the stock, stir in the garlic, the beans with their liquid, and three-quarters of the tarragon, then cover and simmer for 15 mins or until the veg is just tender. Stir in the remaining tarragon before serving.

White velvet soup with smoky almonds

Prep:10 mins **Cook:**25 mins

Serves 2

Ingredients

- 2 tsp rapeseed oil
- 2 large garlic cloves , sliced
- 2 leeks , trimmed so they're mostly white in colour, washed well, then sliced (about 240g)
- 200g cauliflower , chopped
- 2 tsp vegetable bouillon powder

- 400g cannellini beans , rinsed
- fresh nutmeg , for grating
- 100ml whole milk
- 25g whole almonds , chopped
- ½ tsp smoked paprika
- 2 x 25g slices rye bread , to serve

Method

STEP 1

Heat the oil in a large pan. Add the garlic, leeks and cauliflower and cook for about 5 mins, stirring frequently, until starting to soften (but not colouring).

STEP 2

Stir in the vegetable bouillon and beans, pour in 600ml boiling water and add a few generous gratings of the nutmeg. Cover and leave to simmer for 15 mins until the leeks and cauliflower are tender. Add the milk and blitz with a hand blender until smooth and creamy.

STEP 3

Put the almonds in a dry pan and cook very gently for 1 min, or until toasted, then remove from the heat. Scatter the paprika over the almonds and mix well. Ladle the soup into bowls, top with the spicy nuts and serve with the rye bread.

Polish apple cake (Szarlotka)

Prep:35 mins **Cook:**1 hr plus freezing

Serves 12

Ingredients

For the filling

- half a lemon
- 6 large Bramley or cooking apples
- 4 tbsp soft brown sugar
- 1 tbsp ground cinnamon

For the dough

- 450g plain flour , plus extra for dusting
- 1 tsp baking powder
- 200g unsalted butter , cut into pieces, plus extra for greasing
- 225g golden caster sugar
- 3 egg yolks , plus 1 whole egg, at room temperature
- 1 tbsp natural yogurt
- 1 tbsp lemon zest (from the half a lemon, above)
- 1 tsp vanilla extract

To serve

- icing sugar , for dusting
- 300ml pot whipping cream
- 1 tsp cinnamon

Method

STEP 1

Heat oven to 180C/160C fan/gas 4. Grease and line a 20 x 29cm baking tray with baking parchment.

STEP 2

For the filling, zest the lemon half and leave aside for the dough. Peel, core and thinly slice the apples, then squeeze over the juice of the lemon to stop the fruit turning brown. Put the apples in a large pan and add the sugar, 200ml water and cinnamon. Cook for 5 mins, then remove from the heat and leave to cool in the liquid (you'll need this later).

STEP 3

To make the dough, put the flour and baking powder in a food processor or into a large bowl and pulse or stir to combine. Add the butter and mix again until the mixture is sandy. Add the sugar, egg yolks and egg, yogurt, lemon zest and vanilla extract and mix into a dough. Tip it out onto a floured surface. Bring it together with your hands and roll it into a ball.

STEP 4

Split the dough in half, wrap one half in cling film and freeze for 1 hr. Roll out the other dough half so that it is big enough to fill the bottom of the lined tray. With the palm of your hand, push the dough about halfway up the sides of the tray until the whole base is covered. Prick the dough with a fork and bake in the oven for about 15 mins until it is golden and lightly springy to the touch.

STEP 5

Spoon over the apple filling, with about half the cooking liquid, then set aside.

STEP 6

Remove the dough from the freezer and coarsely grate, as you would a block of cheese. Sprinkle the grated dough over the apples and bake for 40-45 mins until it is golden and the topping has cooked through. Leave to cool completely, dust with icing sugar, then cut into squares. Whip the cream until thick, stir in the cinnamon and serve alongside the cake.

Vegan bolognese

Prep:20 mins **Cook:**1 hr

Serves 3

Ingredients

- 15g dried porcini mushrooms
- 1 ½ tbsp olive oil
- ½ onion, finely chopped
- 1 carrot, finely chopped
- 1 celery stick, finely chopped
- 2 garlic cloves, sliced
- 2 thyme sprigs
- ½ tsp tomato purée
- 50ml vegan red wine (optional)
- 125g dried green lentils
- 400g can whole plum tomatoes
- 125g chestnut mushrooms, chopped
- 125g portobello mushrooms, sliced
- ½ tsp soy sauce
- ½ tsp Marmite
- 270g spaghetti
- handful fresh basil leaves

Method

STEP 1

Pour 400ml boiling water over the dried porcini and leave for 10 mins until hydrated. Meanwhile pour 1 tbsp oil into a large saucepan. Add the onion, carrot, celery and a pinch of salt. Cook gently, stirring for 10 mins until soft. Remove the porcini from the liquid, keeping the mushroomy stock and roughly chop. Set both aside.

STEP 2

Add the garlic and thyme to the pan. Cook for 1 min then stir in the tomato purée and cook for a min more. Pour in the red wine, if using, cook until nearly reduced, then add the lentils, reserved mushroom stock and tomatoes. Bring to the boil, then reduce the heat and leave to simmer with a lid on.

STEP 3

Meanwhile, heat a large frying pan. Add the remaining oil, then tip in the chestnut, portobello and rehydrated mushrooms. Fry until all the water has evaporated and the mushrooms are deep golden brown. Pour in the soy sauce. Give everything a good mix, then scrape the mushrooms into the lentil mixture.

STEP 4

Stir in the Marmite and continue to cook the ragu, stirring occasionally, over a low-medium heat for 30-45 mins until the lentils are cooked and the sauce is thick and reduced, adding extra water if necessary. Remove the thyme sprigs and season to taste.

STEP 5

Cook the spaghetti in a large pan of salted water for 1 min less than packet instructions. Drain the pasta, reserving a ladleful of pasta water, then toss the spaghetti in the sauce, using a little of the starchy liquid to loosen up the ragu slightly so that the pasta clings to the sauce. Serve topped with fresh basil and some black pepper.

Simple sugar roses

Total time 1 hr Takes 1 hour per batch. no cook

Makes 40 roses and leaves

Ingredients

edible food colouring paste (we used Claret and Party Green)

200g ready-to-roll icing

a little solid vegetable fat, for rolling (see Know-how below)

edible lustre (we used a shimmery pink), optional

edible sparkles (we used bright pink), optional

Method

STEP 1

Start with the roses. Knead a little of the colouring paste into 150g of the icing until pale and even. Break into three balls, then add a little more colouring to two, giving three varying depths of colour. Keep under cling film. Rub a very thin layer of fat over a smooth work surface. Roll out one of the balls of icing thinly, about 1-2mm, then trim into a rectangle about 8 x 20cm. Cut off a 1cm strip of icing widthways, keeping the rest covered.

STEP 2

Carefully roll the icing up and around itself. For a more realistic rose look, start rolling slightly skew-whiff so that the outside edge of the finished rose sticks out further than the middle. With about 2cm to go, start to guide the end of the icing down and under to make a neat rosebud. Pinch to shape, then cut or pinch off the bottom. Set aside for at least 1 hr until firm. Repeat with the rest of the icing.

STEP 3

For the leaves, colour the remaining icing green. Pinch off small pea-size pieces, roll into balls, then flatten a little. Pinch one end to make a leaf shape. Leave to dry.

STEP 4

Once the roses are dry and firm, dust a little lustre onto each rose using a paintbrush or your fingertip. Sprinkle with sparkles, if using. Position the roses onto the cupcakes in clusters of three, following with three leaves. You'll need 36 leaves and roses for 12 cakes.

Avocado & strawberry smoothie

Prep:5 mins No cook

Serves 2

Ingredients

- ½ avocado , stoned, peeled and cut into chunks
- 150g strawberry , halved
- 4 tbsp low-fat natural yogurt
- 200ml semi-skimmed milk
- lemon or lime juice , to taste
- honey , to taste

Method

STEP 1

Put all the ingredients in a blender and whizz until smooth. If the consistency is too thick, add a little water.

Samosa pie

Prep:5 mins **Cook:**30 mins

Serves 4

Ingredients

- 2-3 tbsp vegetable oil
- 1 onion , chopped
- 500g lamb mince
- 2 garlic cloves , finely chopped
- 2 tbsp curry powder
- 1 large sweet potato (about 300g), peeled and grated
- 100g frozen peas
- handful coriander , roughly chopped
- juice 0.5 lemon
- 3-4 sheets filo pastry
- 1 tsp cumin seeds

Method

STEP 1

Heat oven to 180C/160C fan/gas 4. Heat 1 tbsp of the oil in a frying pan. Cook the onion and mince for about 5 mins until the meat is browned. Stir in the garlic, curry powder, sweet potato and 300ml water. Cook for 5-8 mins until the potato has softened. Stir in the peas, coriander and a squeeze of lemon juice, then season.

STEP 2

Spoon the mixture into a baking dish. Brush the sheets of filo with the remaining oil and scrunch over the top of the mince. Sprinkle with cumin seeds and bake for 10-15 mins or until the top is crisp.

Gooseberry crème brûlée tart

Prep:10 mins **Cook:**1 hr and 20 mins

Serves 8

Ingredients

- 450g gooseberries
- 200g white caster sugar
- 4 eggs
- 100ml double cream
- 500g block sweet pastry
- flour , for dusting

Method

STEP 1

Tip the gooseberries into a saucepan with 100g of the sugar and 100ml water. Simmer for 8-10 mins until the fruit is soft and the juices are syrupy. Tip the fruit into a sieve set over a jug and leave to strain – you will need about 150ml of the syrupy juices. Tip the pulp into a bowl and leave to cool.

STEP 2

In a separate bowl, beat the eggs with 50g of the sugar, then beat in the cream and gooseberry syrup. Strain through a sieve into another jug and set aside.

STEP 3

Heat oven to 160C/140C fan/gas 3. Roll out the pastry on a lightly floured surface to the thickness of a £1 coin, then lift into a 23cm tart tin. Press down gently on the bottom and sides, leaving a slight overhang. Line the tart with foil and fill with baking beans. Bake for 10 mins, then discard the foil and beans, and bake for another 20 mins. Remove from the oven and leave to cool.

STEP 4

Reduce oven to 150C/130C fan/gas 2. Spread the pulp evenly over the base of the tart, then carefully pour the cream mixture over it to create 2 layers. Bake for 35-40 mins until the cream layer has the slightest wobble to it. Remove from the oven and trim the pastry edges. Leave to cool completely, then scatter over the remaining sugar, caramelise with a blowtorch, if you like, and serve straight away.

Red pepper & bean tikka masala

Prep:10 mins **Cook:**20 mins

Serves 2

Ingredients

- 1 tbsp vegetable oil
- 1 onion , chopped
- 2 red peppers , deseeded and cut into strips
- 1 garlic clove , crushed
- thumb-sized piece of ginger , grated
- 1 red chilli , finely chopped
- ½ tbsp garam masala
- ½ tbsp curry powder
- 1 tbsp tomato purée
- 415g can baked beans
- ½ lemon , juiced
- rice and coriander, to serve

Method

STEP 1

Heat the oil in a saucepan over a medium heat, add the onion and red peppers with a pinch of salt and fry until softened, around 5 mins. Tip in the garlic, ginger and red chilli along with the spices and fry for a couple of mins longer.

STEP 2

Spoon in the tomato purée, stir, then tip in the baked beans along with 100ml water. Bubble for 5 mins, then squeeze in the lemon juice. Serve with the rice and scatter over the coriander leaves.

Basic curried roast chickpeas

Prep:5 mins **Cook:**20 mins

Serves 4

Ingredients

- 2 x 400g cans chickpeas
- 1½ tbsp rapeseed oil
- 1 tsp caraway seeds
- 1 tsp mustard seeds
- 1 tbsp curry powder

Method

STEP 1

Heat oven to 200C/180C fan/gas 6. Drain the chickpeas and pat with a tea towel to remove as much moisture as possible. Tip them onto a roasting tray, toss with the oil, seeds and seasoning and roast for 20 mins until golden brown. Toss in the curry powder and enjoy.

Lentil & cauliflower curry

Prep:10 mins **Cook:**40 mins

Serves 4

Ingredients

- 1 tbsp olive oil
- 1 large onion, chopped
- 3 tbsp curry paste
- 1 tsp turmeric
- 1 tsp mustard seeds
- 200g red or yellow lentil
- 1l low-sodium vegetable or chicken stock (made with 2 cubes)
- 1 large cauliflower, broken into florets
- 1 large potato, diced
- 3 tbsp coconut yogurt
- small pack coriander, chopped
- juice 1 lemon
- 100g cooked brown rice

Method

STEP 1

Heat the oil in a large saucepan and cook the onion until soft, about 5 mins. Add the curry paste, spices and lentils, then stir to coat the lentils in the onions and paste. Pour over the stock and simmer for 20 mins, then add the cauliflower, potato and a little extra water if it looks a bit dry.

STEP 2

Simmer for about 12 mins until the cauliflower and potatoes are tender. Stir in the yogurt, coriander and lemon juice, and serve with the brown rice.

Spicy chicken & bean stew

Prep:15 mins **Cook:**1 hr and 20 mins

Serves 6

Ingredients

- 1¼ kg chicken thighs and drumsticks (approx. weight, we used a 1.23kg mixed pack)
- 1 tbsp olive oil
- 2 onions, sliced

- 1 garlic clove, crushed
- 2 red chillies, deseeded and chopped
- 250g frozen peppers, defrosted
- 400g can chopped tomatoes
- 420g can kidney beans in chilli sauce
- 2 x 400g cans butter beans, drained
- 400ml hot chicken stock
- small bunch coriander, chopped
- 150ml pot soured cream and crusty bread, to serve

Method

STEP 1

Pull the skin off the chicken and discard. Heat the oil in a large casserole dish, brown the chicken all over, then remove with a slotted spoon. Tip in the onions, garlic and chillies, then fry for 5 mins until starting to soften and turn golden.

STEP 2

Add the peppers, tomatoes, beans and hot stock. Put the chicken back on top, half-cover with a pan lid and cook for 50 mins, until the chicken is cooked through and tender.

STEP 3

Stir through the coriander and serve with soured cream and crusty bread.

Orange & raspberry granola

Prep:15 mins **Cook:**25 mins plus at least 1 hr chilling

Serves 4

Ingredients

- 400g jumbo oats
- juice 2 oranges (150ml), plus zest of 1/2
- 1 tsp ground cinnamon
- 2 tbsp freeze-dried raspberries or strawberries (see tip)
- 25g flaked almonds , toasted

- 25g mixed seeds (such as sunflower, pumpkin, sesame and linseed)

To serve

- 2 large oranges , peeled and segmented
- mint leaves (optional)

Method

STEP 1

Put 200g oats and 500ml water in a food processor and blitz for 1 min. Line a sieve with clean muslin and pour in the oat mixture. Leave to drip through for 5 mins, then twist the ends of the muslin and squeeze well to capture as much of the oat milk as possible – it should be the consistency of single cream. Best chilled at least 1 hr before serving. Can be kept in a sealed or covered jug in the fridge for up to 3 days.

STEP 2

Heat oven to 200C/180C fan/gas 6 and line a baking tray with baking parchment. Put the orange juice in a medium saucepan and bring to the boil. Boil rapidly for 5 mins or until the liquid has reduced by half, stirring occasionally. Mix the remaining 200g oats with the orange zest and cinnamon. Remove the pan from the heat and stir the oat mixture into the juice. Spread over the lined tray in a thin layer and bake for 10-15 mins or until lightly browned and crisp, turning the oats every few mins. Leave to cool on the tray.

STEP 3

Once cool, mix the oats with the raspberries, flaked almonds and seeds. Can be kept in a sealed jar for up to one week. To serve, spoon the granola into bowls, pour over the oat milk and top with the orange segments and mint leaves, if you like.

Herby chicken gyros

Prep:10 mins **Cook:**4 mins

Serves 2

Ingredients

- 1 large skinless chicken breast
- rapeseed oil , for brushing

- small garlic clove , crushed
- ½ tsp dried oregano
- 2 tbsp Greek yogurt
- 10 cm piece cucumber , grated, excess juice squeezed out
- 2 tbsp chopped mint , plus a few leaves to serve
- 2 wholemeal pitta breads
- 2 red or yellow tomatoes , sliced
- 1 red pepper from a jar (not in oil), deseeded and sliced

Method

STEP 1

Cut the chicken breast in half lengthways, then cover with cling film and bash with a rolling pin to flatten it. Brush with some oil, then cover with the garlic, oregano and some pepper. Heat a non-stick frying pan and cook the chicken for a few mins each side. Meanwhile, mix the yogurt, cucumber and mint to make tzatziki.

STEP 2

Cut the tops from the pittas along their longest side and stuff with the chicken, tomato, pepper and tzatziki. Poke in a few mint leaves to serve. If taking to the office for lunch, pack the tzatziki in a separate pot and add just before eating to prevent the pitta going soggy before lunchtime.

Roast roots with goat's cheese & spinach

Prep:30 mins **Cook:**55 mins

Serves 2

Ingredients

- 350g butternut squash , deseeded and cut into chunks, peeled if you like
- 200g carrots , peeled and cut into long batons
- 250g parsnips , peeled and cut into long batons
- 200g raw beetroot , well-scrubbed and cut into thick wedges
- 1 medium red onion , cut into wedges
- 1 tbsp cold-pressed rapeseed oil
- juice and finely grated zest 1 lemon

- 1 bulb garlic , cloves separated
- 4-5 thyme sprigs , leaves roughly chopped
- 75g soft rindless goat's cheese log
- 25g mixed nuts , such as brazils, almonds, hazelnuts, pecans and walnuts, roughly chopped
- 50g baby leaf spinach

Method

STEP 1

Heat oven to 200C/180C fan/gas 6. Put the vegetables, without the garlic, into a bowl and toss with the oil, lemon zest and juice and plenty of ground black pepper.

STEP 2

Scatter the vegetables over a large baking tray or roasting tin and bake for 30 mins. Take the tray out of the oven, add the garlic and thyme, then turn the vegetables. Return to the oven for 20 mins or until the vegetables are tender and lightly browned, turning halfway through. Dot with the goat's cheese and nuts, scatter over the spinach and return to the oven for 3-5 mins or until the spinach has wilted and the goat's cheese has begun to melt. You can press the softened garlic cloves out of their skins and mash with the roasted vegetables, if you like.

Spice-crusted aubergines & peppers with pilaf

Prep:10 mins **Cook:**30 mins

Serves 4

Ingredients

- 2 large aubergines , halved
- 2 tbsp extra virgin olive oil
- 2 red peppers , quartered
- 2 tsp ground cinnamon
- 2 tsp chilli flakes
- 2 tsp za'atar
- 4 tbsp pomegranate molasses
- 140g puy lentils
- 140g basmati rice
- seeds from 1 pomegranate

- small pack flat-leaf parsley , roughly chopped
- Greek or coconut yogurt , to serve

Method

STEP 1

Heat oven to 220C/200C fan/gas 7. Using a sharp knife, score a diamond pattern into the aubergines. Brush with 1 tbsp of the oil, season well and place on a baking tray, cut-side down. Cook in the oven for 15 mins. Add the peppers to the tray, turn the aubergines over and drizzle everything with the remaining oil. Sprinkle over the spices, 1 tbsp of the pomegranate molasses and a little salt. Roast in the oven for 15 mins more.

STEP 2

Boil the lentils in plenty of water until al dente. After they've been boiling for 5 mins, add the rice. Cook for 10 mins or until cooked through but with a bit of bite. Drain and return to the pan, covered with a lid to keep warm.

STEP 3

Stir the pomegranate seeds and parsley through the lentil rice. Divide between four plates or tip onto a large platter. Top with the roasted veg, a dollop of yogurt and the remaining pomegranate molasses drizzled over.

Potato pancakes with chard & eggs

Prep:10 mins **Cook:**15 mins

Serves 2

Ingredients

- 300g mashed potato
- 4 spring onions , very finely chopped
- 25g plain wholemeal flour
- ½ tsp baking powder
- 3 eggs
- 2 tsp rapeseed oil
- 240g chard , stalks and leaves roughly chopped, or baby spinach, chopped

Method

STEP 1

Mix the mash, spring onions, flour, baking powder and 1 of the eggs in a bowl. Heat the oil in a non-stick frying pan, then spoon in the potato mix to make two mounds. Flatten them to form two 15cm discs and fry for 5-8 mins until the undersides are set and golden, then carefully ip over and cook on the other side.

STEP 2

Meanwhile, wash the chard and put in a pan with some of the water still clinging to it, then cover and cook over a medium heat for 5 mins until wilted and tender. Poach the remaining eggs.

STEP 3

Top the pancakes with the greens and egg. Serve while the yolks are still runny.